The WORST-CASE SCENARIO Business Survival Guide

The WORST-CASE SCENARIO Business Survival Guide

How to Survive the Recession,
Handle Layoffs, Raise Emergency Cash,
Thwart an Employee Coup,
and Avoid Other Potential Disasters!

David Borgenicht and Mark Joyner
New York Times Best-selling Authors

WILEY

John Wiley & Sons, Inc.

Illustrations by Colin Hayes

Visit www.worstcasebusiness.com for updates, free resources, and more!

Published by John Wiley & Sons, Inc., Hoboken, New Jersey
Published simultaneously in Canada

For general information on our other products and services or for technical support, please contact our Customer Care Department within the United States at (800) 762-2974, outside the United States at (317) 572-3993 or fax (317) 572-4002.

Wiley also publishes its books in a variety of electronic formats. Some content that appears in print may not be available in electronic books. For more information about Wiley products, visit our web site at www.wiley.com.

ISBN: 978-0-470-55141-7

Printed in the United States of America

10 9 8 7 6 5 4 3 2 1

If you're going through Hell, keep going.

Winston Churchill

CONTENTS

Mark's Introduction

When you're in business, things are going to go wrong. Terribly wrong. And often. These things-gone-wrong reveal two classes of entrepreneur: those who charge on despite things-gone-wrong, and those who punk out.

The good news is that these are learned behaviors, not inborn traits. But here's the problem: A good portion of learning to "charge on" comes from the confidence of knowing that you will know what to do when things go wrong. The paradox is that such knowledge tends to come from experience. So, what do you do?

The answer is easy: Keep this guide with you. Then charge on, with the knowledge that nearly every potentially business-killing situation has a solution. You can rest easy because the solutions in these pages have been battle-tested by business titans of the ages.

If I had such a resource when I was starting my first business, I would have been spared a tremendous amount of pain and suffering. My wish is that, with this advice, you will far surpass even my greatest business triumphs.

There are a few core lessons every entrepreneur must learn, and we've distilled them for you in the Basic Training sections and epilogue. I urge you to read them now; then use this book as an arms-reach resource for the future.

Charge on.

Mark Joyner
mark@worstcasebusiness.com

David's Introduction

Let me start by confessing that I am not a business guru.

Yes, I am the creator and coauthor of one of the best-selling brands in recent publishing (heck—all publishing) history—The Worst-Case Scenario franchise.

Sure, I run a decently successful book publishing company—Quirk Books (www.quirkbooks.com)—which is tough to say these days.

But I am not a multimillionaire. I do not make my living as a business coach, consultant, or savior. I haven't gone to business school, I never got an MBA, and I haven't (yet) sold my garage startup for hundreds of millions of dollars or invented dozens of infomercial-worthy devices with "Magic" in the name.

And yet, I can tell you, without any sense of humor or irony, both from personal and professional experience, this book just might save your business.

Speaking not as an author but as a small-business owner who has been through all kinds of worst-case scenarios—from extreme cash tightness to enacting layoffs, from the perils of "mission drift" to the dreaded "feature creep," from deadbeat customers to miserable employees—I can tell you that the clear, straightforward, step-by-step information within *The Worst-Case Scenario Business Survival Guide* is just the resource you'll need when your business suddenly takes a turn for the worse.

And I can tell you that this book is no joke.

Whereas the other Worst-Case Scenario books I've worked on have been meant more for entertainment and humor than actual survival value, this book is truly essential reading for any business owner. My coauthor, Mark Joyner, and I have worked hard to identify and find the answers to dozens of the toughest situations that you as a business owner will ever face—and to provide you with the training necessary to ensure you never face them again. Plus, we've solicited dozens of business experts to contribute their knowledge to help you make it through.

It could well be the most valuable business book you will buy.

After all, when a worst-case scenario happens, you don't want pages and pages of anecdotes or fables or statistics or tons of heavily charts and diagrams. You want answers. Fast. That's what makes this book unique. We get right to the meat of the matter—the step-by-step answers you're looking for to help you and your business survive the crisis that is happening to you now.

It's a resource I wish I'd had when dealing with many of these same situations. I'm glad we made it through, and I'm glad we've found a way to bring it to you, via the good people at Wiley.

Now, I can't promise that all the answers you will ever require are within these pages. Depending on your specific situation, you may need to adjust here or there. You may need to change the order of the steps you take, depending on your industry, culture, or business model.

But I can promise you that if you remain calm, if you don't give in to panic, if you prepare for the worst, and if you make a plan for what comes next, you and your business will survive.

Good luck. And I hope to hear from you on the other side.

David Borgenicht
david@worstcasebusiness.com

Chapter 1
Financial Emergencies

HOW TO SURVIVE WHEN YOU CAN'T MAKE PAYROLL

Expert Adviser

John Paul DeJoria, www.paulmitchell.com

---

❶ ANNOUNCE AN IMMEDIATE SPENDING AND HIRING FREEZE.

The freeze should include salaries, entertainment, unnecessary travel—any expenditure that will not negatively affect your cash flow or profitability. Your management team should sign off on all expenses.

GET BACK TO YOUR ROOTS.

Return to when you first started your business—when you didn't have the human resources and/or funds that you have now—and run your business based on the same ideals as you did then. Use the minimum resources, as you did to survive in the beginning, and you will stay afloat. Be strategic about which practices you revert to, however; for example, if more than 50 percent of your clientele comes from advertising on billboards, do not stop the advertising.

❸ CUT OUT THE WEAK LINKS IN YOUR TEAM.

Use this opportunity to shed problem employees and/or those who are not pulling their weight. Tell them that you're sorry, but you have to lay them off due to economic conditions. (Remember that a layoff is easier to defend legally than a firing is, so you're dodging a potential legal bullet as well.)

❹ REDUCE SALARIES OF OVERPAID EMPLOYEES.

Define overpaid as anyone on your executive team (including you) whom you could replace for more than a 10 percent salary savings. Explain that you have two options:

- To lay them off
- To keep them but to cut their pay

You must be prepared to reduce your own compensation at least as much as the reductions to the salaries of other employees.

❺ IF AN ESSENTIAL EXECUTIVE LEAVES, FIND AN EQUALLY COMPETENT REPLACEMENT WHO WILL WORK FOR LESS.

They are always out there.

❻ ENLIST EVERYONE IN THE EFFORT TO CUT EXPENSES FURTHER AND BRING IN MORE REVENUE.

Explain the reality of the situation to your employees. Empathize with how it affects them personally and tell them how it affects you personally as well. Then state that you don't want to lay off any more staff, but that in order to avoid doing so you need their help.

7 DO NOT LIE, PANIC, OR ACT HELPLESS.

If you lie you will be found out, and no amount of cash will save you. Be completely open and honest with all parties (employees, vendors, clients). If you panic, the rest of your company will follow suit. And if you act helpless, your team will lose respect and focus.

8 ENGAGE EVERYONE IN "EMERGENCY CASH FLOW" PROCEDURES.

9 PROPOSE ACROSS-THE-BOARD PAY CUTS.

Explain that all staff must take a pay cut to avoid layoffs.

10 IF YOU'RE STILL BLEEDING CASH, ENACT LAYOFFS.

See page 46.

11 DO NOT GIVE UP.

The difference between successful people and unsuccessful people is that successful people do all the things unsuccessful people do not want to do. If thirty-nine doors have been slammed in your face, be as enthusiastic on the fortieth door as you were on the first. Persistence is the key to success.

HOW TO PERFORM EMERGENCY SURGERY ON YOUR OVERHEAD

Expert Adviser
Dan Kuschell, www.dankuschell.com

---

❶ IMMEDIATELY ENACT PAY AND EXPENSE FREEZES.
Do not allow additional expenses to be authorized without the approval of a department manager.

❷ DETERMINE IMMEDIATE PRIORITIES AND GOALS.
Verify whether your business is merely in a period of significant cash tightness or if it's a true emergency situation ("survival" mode). Identify short-term goals and proceed accordingly. For example, if you can't cover your expenses now, it may not be important to continue spending on the development of products that won't reach the market until the next year.

❸ ELIMINATE ALL NONESSENTIAL AND SPECULATIVE EXPENSES FIRST.

Slash these immediately: discretionary expenses and travel, entertainment, and marketing expenses.

❹ IDENTIFY YOUR BUSINESS'S MAJOR OVERHEAD EXPENSES.

These include such things as telephone service, office supplies, printing costs, cleaning services, shipping fees, insurance, payroll, banking fees, and leases.

❺ RECOGNIZE THAT VIRTUALLY EVERYTHING IS NEGOTIABLE, EVEN IF PREVIOUSLY NEGOTIATED.

You might think that your suppliers and vendors give you the best deal upfront, but it is smart business to regularly shop their competitors to keep them on their toes—especially in a time of need. Remember that you can not only negotiate how much you pay for something but also when you need to pay for it.

Be pigheaded and stubborn and track down the best options for your business.

❻ REDUCE PHONE EXPENSES.

Cell phones and landlines can quickly run up your bills. Technology has advanced dramatically. Monitor your cellphone minutes to identify which is the best plan for you. In addition, consider converting traditional phone service to a VOIP service. Be sure that your agreement states that you are automatically grandfathered into any future rate

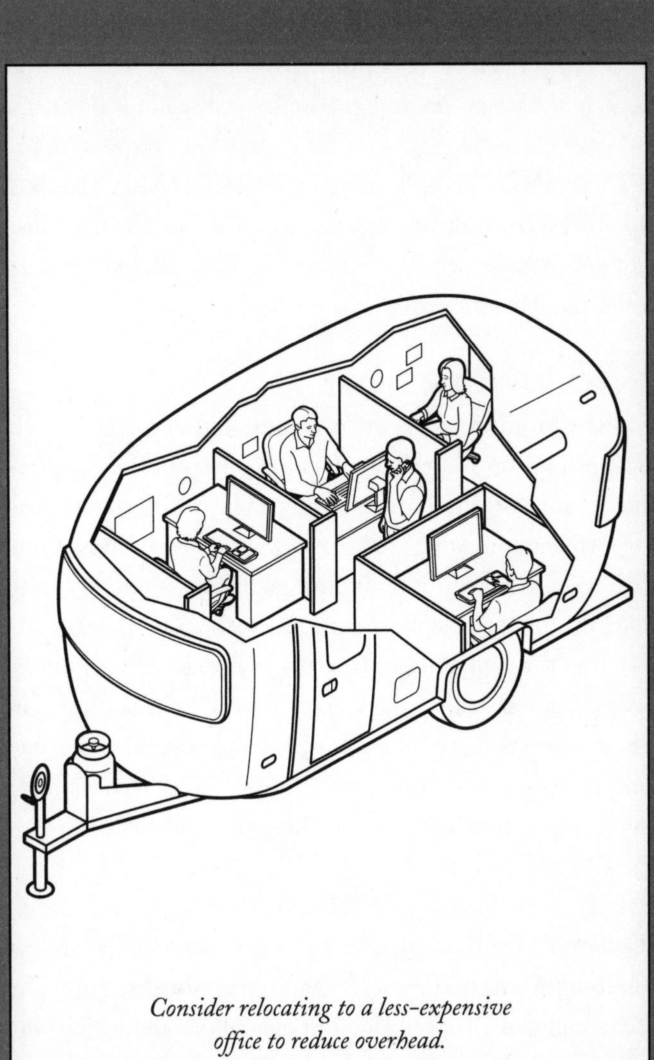

Consider relocating to a less-expensive office to reduce overhead.

reduction or bulk savings. The service provider wins because you will remain their customer, and you win because you lock in the best rates and get the same discounts as others.

7 FIND AND JOIN A GROUP PURCHASE PLAN.

Identify a company or organization that benefits from discounts on major services/products, and you can benefit from their purchase power.

8 INVOLVE YOUR TEAM.

Create an initiative to involve your staff and solicit their suggestions on ways they can cut expenses in their department, area, or division. Engaging them will foster a sense of ownership in what they do and, more important, establish a focus on profitability. Engage your teams to create budgets for their departments. Enlist them in understanding that the goal of their department is to be a profit center as well, and that the goal is to achieve a 10-to-1 return on their expenses. Doing so will result in an awareness that you are in business to earn a profit. It also encourages team responsibil-ity and a focus on making smart choices.

9 CUT OUT THE WEAK LINKS.

Determine the weak members on your team and look to cut them back or lay them off. Remove personality from the equation: Consider only job responsibilities and which employees are and are not vital to help you reach your goals.

⑩ COMMUNICATE CLEARLY, HONESTLY, AND OPENLY WITH YOUR TEAM, VENDORS, AND SUPPLIERS.

Always remember to talk about what's in it for them as you explain the outcome you want. In other words, if you end up cutting expenses and taking on more work, you won't have to make further cuts and eventually you will get back on track. When dealing with a vendor or supplier, explain that if they help you, you will guarantee your business to them for a meaningful period. Ultimately, your staff will understand. And your vendors and suppliers want your business.

⑪ NEVER FEEL GUILTY ABOUT ASKING FOR HELP.

Your primary responsibility as a business owner is to earn a profit. That gives you the leverage to create more opportunities for your staff, your growth, and your relationships with vendors, which ultimately means that you are creating more jobs and opportunity in the world.

HOW TO GET CASH FAST

Expert Adviser

Scott Lorenz, www.westwindcos.com

---

❶ BEGIN AN ALL-OUT ASSAULT TO COLLECT RECEIVABLES.

If a firm but polite phone call does not do the trick, consider turning over your overdue receivables to a collections agency. It could get ugly, but so is not paying a debt.

❷ ENGAGE IN EMERGENCY MARKETING METHODS.

There are many possible seasonal and fire-sale-type marketing tactics that you should always be trying. Emergency marketing is just doing what you should be doing all the time, but with a different flair. Do you have unsold inventory? Offer great deals to key customers. Give away three items for the price of two. Offer credit for a future order as a bonus. Run a special on something that costs you very little to produce. If times are truly desperate, you might engage in a "save our company" marketing campaign and request donations. The only limit is your creativity.

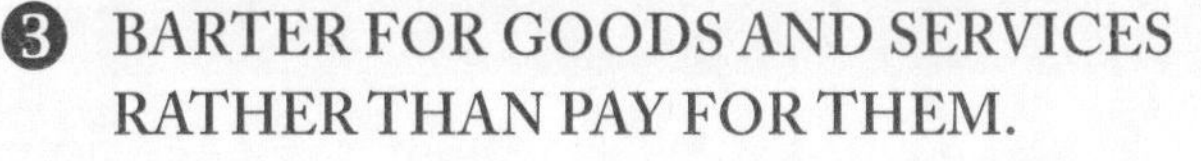

3 BARTER FOR GOODS AND SERVICES RATHER THAN PAY FOR THEM.

Offer key vendors something they value that you can provide (without additional expense) in exchange for the goods and services you need. This can be done with anyone—individual or organizational. Some examples: If your company is an advertising agency, offer to create a free campaign for your IT vendor in exchange for services. If it is a publishing company, offer to create and design a company history coffee-table book for a key client or vendor in exchange for a product or service you need. Think about what you have to offer; then offer it.

4 LOOK FOR HELP FROM OTHERS IN YOUR (OR A RELATED) INDUSTRY WHO ARE ALSO STRUGGLING.

This method will not bring in cash, but it may improve your bottom line by creating affiliate relationships or strategic partnerships. Offer a percentage of your online sales to a group or business that will help you sell your wares. Offer to send another company's e-blast to customers in your database if they send yours to theirs. Be certain there is an affinity in your customer demographic. Such partnerships can be a boon in times of need (and in other times as well).

5 SEEK DEBT-RESTRUCTURING OPPORTUNITIES.

Debt restructuring allows a private or public company—or a sovereign entity—that is facing cash-flow problems and

Use the following methods to accelerate cash flow:

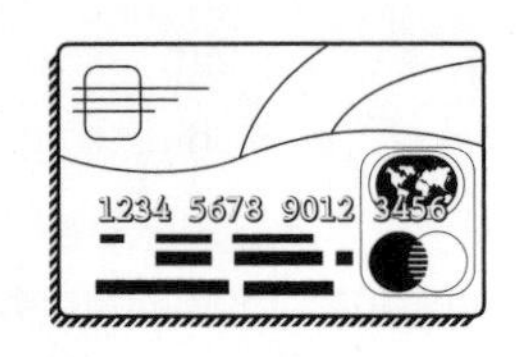

Credit card

Telemarketing campaign

Emergency marketing campaign

Investment/sale of equity

Direct sales

financial distress to reduce and renegotiate its delinquent debts in order to improve or restore liquidity and rehabilitate so that it can continue operations. Many businesses can assist with this process. Google them.

❻ SEEK DEBT-CONSOLIDATION OPPORTUNITIES WITH LENDERS.

You may be able to negotiate a reduction in your initial payment and interest rates in one fell swoop. Approach your existing lenders first and then your creditors. Longtime vendors in sound financial health may be willing to help.

❼ SEEK INVESTORS OR ENGAGE IN A DEBT-FOR-EQUITY EXCHANGE.

Your company may be worth more than you realize—and there may be a shrewd investor out there willing to take advantage of your economic hardship for a piece of the action. Just make sure you do not end up selling out your company in exchange for a job you hate. (Fact: Many people who sell their companies end up becoming the CEO for a pittance. If you want a job, there are easier ways to get one.)

❽ TRY TO OBTAIN A CREDIT LINE FROM YOUR BANK.

Inquire about what your bank can offer. It is often easier than you think, especially if you have good receivables or other collateral.

 APPLY FOR MULTIPLE CREDIT CARDS.

Remember all those “You’ve been preapproved!” notices? Time to start calling them in. Many legendary businesses have been saved (and started) with credit-card financing.

HOW TO COLLECT FROM A DEADBEAT CUSTOMER

1 BE THE SQUEAKY WHEEL—OR, BETTER YET, THE NAILS ON THE CHALKBOARD.

You will not get the attention you need from the A/P department of a deadbeat vendor, so call your main contact first. And do so often. When you reach that person, state that you understand cash-flow problems and that they need to work out a payment plan.

2 CALL WITH A POLITE REMINDER THAT THE BILLING IS DUE.

Say, "I'm sure it must have slipped your mind because you're the kind of person who always pays promptly. Can I take your credit card information for that now?"

CALL AGAIN.

Say, "I'm sure you must be experiencing a tough time over there. Everyone is. Unfortunately, we won't be able to provide your service if we cannot settle the bill. Can I take the payment details from you now?"

4 PROVIDE AN INCENTIVE TO PAY YOU FIRST.

Try the "carrot" approach before attempting the "stick" approach. Offer a discount on future goods or services or a discount on their current payable if they pay you first and agree to give you another order.

5 EXPLORE OTHER OPTIONS.

If the squeaky-wheel approach is still unsuccessful (that is, if you have been unable to make contact or if the vendor has not lived up to its obligations), a stronger course of action is required.

6 CUT OFF SERVICE AND CALL AGAIN.

Say, "Hey, sorry to let you know we've unfortunately had to cut off your service. Would you like to get that restored now?" If you are seeking payment for services already rendered (or products already delivered), say, "I just wanted to see if I can settle your bill. We were really counting on your payment. Can we settle that now?"

7 THREATEN LEGAL ACTION.

Tell the deadbeat customer that you "do not wish this to be turned over to your legal teams to resolve" or that you "do not wish to withhold" their goods or services but that you will be forced to do so if they refuse to pay.

There are plenty of effective, legal solutions to collecting on bad debts.

8. THREATEN NEGATIVE PUBLICITY.

Explain that you are well connected and will spread the word throughout the industry that the company is not paying its bills and should not be trusted. Or threaten to alert the media (major or trade) if the company has some notoriety.

9. IF MULTIPLE ATTEMPTS STILL FAIL, REFER THE ACCOUNT TO A COLLECTION SERVICE.

But be sure to contact the vendor one last time to alert them that you are about to do so. Note that a collector will retain a percentage of the amount collected and should require no upfront payment from you.

Be Aware

Consider building discounts into your budget to ensure that money is received immediately. Provide a discount for a customer if they pay within 30 days or on the spot.

HOW TO RENEGOTIATE WITH YOUR CREDITORS

1. TARGET YOUR BIGGEST CREDITORS FIRST.
Renegotiating your terms/payables with these creditors will make the biggest immediate impact on your cash flow. In addition, because these are the creditors most likely to value your continued business and health, they are thus most likely to want to help you.

2. RULE OUT NO ONE.
Any creditor is an option. Every business wants to be paid for their products and services, and everyone wants your future business.

3. RESEARCH WHAT OTHERS ARE PAYING FOR SIMILAR GOODS AND SERVICES AND DETERMINE IF A BETTER RATE IS AVAILABLE ELSEWHERE.
Knowing this information will not only help you negotiate a better deal with your existing creditors but also provide alternatives should things not work out.

4. IF POSSIBLE, CALL THE CREDITOR BEFORE YOUR PAYMENT IS DUE.

They will appreciate the honesty and advance notice much more than being called after the payment is already late.

5. BE AS HONEST AS POSSIBLE.

Never lie or make excuses about your inability to pay; every business has cash-flow problems. Explain your situation openly and honestly. (But don't reveal that you're in danger of going out of business, of course.) They will appreciate your forthrightness and reward you for it. (See page 184 for a sample speech.)

6. ASK FOR WHAT YOU WANT.

Better terms, cheaper rates, reduced monthly payments—no request is out of bounds. If they value your business and believe that the alternative is to lose that business altogether, they will work hard to help. Bolster your argument by presenting the information you discovered about the market value of their goods or services (thus implying that you may take your business elsewhere).

7. OFFER AN INCENTIVE TO HELP YOU.

These may include a term of exclusivity, longer contract, bartered goods or services from your company, and even a higher price next year for a lower price now.

❽ IF THAT FAILS, EXPLAIN THAT YOU WILL HAVE TO CHOOSE ANOTHER VENDOR.

This simple, direct statement may get them to work a bit harder to remedy your situation. Your future business is your leverage.

Basic Training

THE RULES

- Do not panic!
- Cash flow is your most important asset.
- Cash flow comes from systems.
- Cash flow can be managed.
- Focus on profit exclusively.
- Not all profit is equal.

DO NOT PANIC!

Ever.

You have heard this advice before. This time, let it actually sink in.

As with all truths, it's one thing to intellectually grasp the concept. It's quite another to truly understand and live by it. It's quite easy to panic during times of financial distress. Everyone else seems to be doing it, so we feel it's only natural to do it as well.

Buck the system and remain calm. Your presence of mind will immediately give you an edge over almost everyone else.

To prove it to yourself, simply do the opposite and see what happens.

Panic about everything. Go ahead. Freak out. Do your worst.

We predict:

a. Your ability to think clearly will be seriously impaired.

b. Your team will stop respecting you.

c. You will stop respecting yourself.

d. Someone may just put you out of your misery.

We are not advising you to become the laid-back surfer dude who takes nothing seriously. On the contrary: Take great care in everything you do. Pay attention to detail. Do not lie to yourself about reality. Just think objectively and stop freaking out if you're not getting your way. Instead, do something about it.

CASH FLOW IS YOUR MOST IMPORTANT ASSET.

Cash flow is more stable than cash. Cash flow is more stable than hard assets. Cash flow is the ultimate asset. Here's why.

Cash is inherently unstable. In economic systems that rely on fiat currencies, the value of your money is only that which is agreed by consensus. The paper you own has no inherent value in itself—it is only the promise of future services rendered that makes your paper worth keeping. A cursory look at history will clearly demonstrate that the value of this paper can fluctuate greatly dependent upon the relative standing of the country that stands behind it. To state it bluntly: If you own the Fredonia dollar and the country of Fredonia is overthrown, the first thing the new leadership is likely to do is to establish a new currency, wiping out the value of the previous one. Similarly, if the Fredonia government makes a bone-headed move that devalues their currency, you can see an equal reversal in the value of your cash assets.

Hard assets are also inherently unstable. They are valuable to you only as long as the jack-booted thugs with billy clubs don't take them away. They are also valuable only if maintained in good condition. Houses can depreciate in value. They can also be destroyed by conditions not covered by your insurance. Every single hard asset that you own is at risk of being taken away or destroyed.

Cash flow, on the other hand, can create cash and hard assets at will. If you own a business in the country of Fredonia and that country's currency is suddenly made null or devalued, you can always generate more cash to respond to these changes. If your home is destroyed, you can build a new one with the profit from your cash flow.

But wait, isn't cash flow itself something that can be subverted by various forces (competitors, market conditions, and so on)?

You bet it is. So that means you cannot build up sources of cash flow and rest on your laurels.

What it does mean is that a source of cash flow is:

- more inherently stable (if properly managed).
- more powerful than other assets, because it is the source of other assets.

How does one manage a cash-flow asset?

By understanding that . . .

CASH FLOW COMES FROM SYSTEMS.

Cash flow does not come from hope.
Cash flow does not come from enthusiasm.
Cash flow does not come from good intentions.
Cash flow comes from approaching your business as a system.
Time, energy, and money go in to your system—and a positive return of money comes out (or not).

CASH FLOW CAN BE MANAGED.

Remember that cash flow is dependent upon only two things:

- **incoming cash**
- **outgoing cash**

If your outgoing cash is greater than your incoming cash, you're screwed.

Or are you?

Managing the timing of when an outgoing must be paid, and when you receive money due to you, can fend off impending doom indefinitely . . . if you're clever enough.

You owe $20,000 to a creditor? Well, see, that's a meaningless statement without understanding when that money is owed. Negotiating with a creditor is one of the easiest things to do in the world. If it comes down to either you going bankrupt and never paying them or you paying them later than expected, any intelligent creditor will accept the latter.

Your incomings can be managed as well. The timing of marketing campaigns, the collection of accounts receivable—when you begin to see all of these things as fluid elements in time you'll understand that you have a great deal more freedom and flexibility when fighting off a financial crisis.

⚠ FOCUS ON PROFIT EXCLUSIVELY.

Yes, cash flow is your ultimate asset, but if you are perpetually in the red, you don't own an asset—you own a liability.

Focusing exclusively on the profitability of your business does two wonderful things:

❶ **It focuses your attention on what's important.**

There's a new technology on the market that's all the rage . . . Should you care? Only if it immediately improves your profit.

There's a rumor floating around that one of your competitors may not like you . . . Should you care? Only if it immediately improves your profit.

One of your employees is moonlighting . . . Should you care? Only if it immediately improves your profit.

The answer to all these questions is another question: Will it impact profitability?

❷ **It renders you immune to the words of business false-profits.**

Before hiring those consultants for a round of whoop-de-doo kumbaya tree hugging, ask yourself if what they advise will impact profitability. Further: Can they prove it?

What profitable businesses have they built?

What businesses have shown a clear improvement in profitability by following their advice?

If the answer is none, then move on.

⚠ NOT ALL PROFIT IS EQUAL.

If you think profit is all about ruthless cutthroat dog-eat-dog profiteering despite the consequence, think again.

Profit should be obtained by one thing and one thing only: creating value.

Yes, many people make money with a number of unhealthy methods: knocking off competitors, stealing ideas, shell-game trades, and all manners of assorted dirty tricks.

Yes, these things can make people a lot of money, but our experience shows that it always leads to ruin. If they do not end up in jail, they will end up in the prison that is a life without true friends. Or worse: the prison that is your own conscience knowing that you are living at the expense of others.

If you think this is nothing more than moral posturing or that it has anything to do with karma or other such mysticism, think again. It's a purely empirical fact based on observation of human behavior.

It's as simple as this: If you can create profit by creating something of true value, not only will you be financially stable but you will sleep well at night. If there is anything more important than that, we don't know what it is.

COLD LEMONADE
50 ¢

Chapter 2
HR Emergencies

HOW TO ENACT AND SURVIVE LAYOFFS

Expert Advisers

Jon Gordon, www.jongordon.com

Kerry Patterson, www.lifetips.com/expert-guru/6189-kerry-patterson.html

---

1 BE HONEST AND OPEN WITH EVERYONE ABOUT THE COMPANY'S SITUATION BEFORE DOING ANYTHING.

This does not mean you need to tell people that you are considering layoffs a month before you enact them. It does mean that your staff should understand the company is struggling, cash is tight, and you are working on solutions. Such openness and transparency will make the act itself less of a surprise when the time comes.

2 PLAN THE LAYOFF DAY COMPLETELY, TO MINIMIZE THE STRESS ON EVERYONE.

Most companies enact layoffs near or at the end of the week. Some companies do their layoffs and firing on Fridays so that the staff has a couple days off before returning to the office, their anxieties, and survivor guilt. Others prefer to hire and fire on Wednesday or Thursday to allow their team to have access to you and other managers and executives for questions, and to just "get back to work."

❸ ACT AS THOUGH EVERYONE IS WATCHING YOU.

Because they will be. Remember that layoffs do not just affect the people you're letting go—they affect those whom you are keeping as well. Everyone will be watching to gauge how you deal with the people being laid off. Are you compassionate? Are you trustworthy? Are you transparent? If you remember to be these things, and act accordingly, your employees will make it through this difficult time more quickly. Know that they will be asking themselves if they can trust you. If your actions tell them that they cannot, then your layoffs will cause morale, productivity, and performance to plummet. Creating a crisis of confidence and lack of trust among the remaining employees could have a disastrous effect on the future of your organization and your team.

❹ BE SWIFT AND COMPLETE.

Termination should not be a long process. Get to the point. Explain that you're sorry, that you have to let people go, and that the position is being eliminated. Be compassionate: Do not treat the people you are laying off like a number. If you talk to each individual and treat them right, the people you retain will treat you in kind. Offer support, guidance, coaching, encouragement, and hope. (See page 178 for a sample speech.)

FEEL PAIN WHEN YOU DELIVER PAIN.

You expect employees to be loyal to you; now is your chance to show loyalty in return by demonstrating your willingness to suffer with them. Do not be afraid to share how agonizing it is for you while sympathizing with their plight. However, before doing anything, make sure your actions are completely sincere.

6 RESPOND TO ANGER WITH COMPASSION.

You can say, "I've done my best to act in the best possible way I could. I am sorry for the turmoil this will cause you and assure you I will help your transition any way I can." Although this statement will not take away the pain, at least it helps you to avoid causing more pain.

7 REPLACE GENERALIZATIONS AND PLATITUDES WITH SPECIFIC COMMITMENTS.

Offer your own support, which is often more personal and meaningful when you are the one sharing the bad news. Your willingness to sacrifice for those leaving is the determinant of how much trust you will garner among those remaining. A specific offer of two or three things that you can do for the individuals you are laying off will reveal a lot more about your sincerity than general "If there's anything I can do" statements.

8 EXPLAIN THE SEVERANCE AND THEN USHER THE INDIVIDUAL OFF THE PREMISES.

Explain that they can arrange a time to come back and pack up their belongings and say their goodbyes—that you will be meeting with the staff immediately to explain what has happened. Letting them pack up at that moment, in front of your staff, will only prolong the agony and make everyone feel embarrassed and awkward.

9 ADDRESS OR COMMUNICATE TO YOUR STAFF IMMEDIATELY AFTERWARD.

Be prepared with a speech. (See page 180 for a sample.)

10 BE COMPLETELY TRANSPARENT WHEN EXPLAINING THE LAYOFFS.

Let people know exactly where the organization stands. Share your rationale behind your decision (including why you chose those you did). When people understand the situation, they are more likely to accept it.

11 DO NOT TORTURE YOUR STAFF WITH MULTIPLE ROUNDS OF LAYOFFS.

Plan to do it once and move on. Err on the side of caution: It is better to have to hire someone in the next six months than to fire more people.

HOW TO FIRE SOMEONE

Expert Advisers

Chris Brogan, www.chrisbrogan.com

Greg Pain, www.biosport.co.nz

Mike Hill, www.mikehillsblog.com

---

❶ PICK THE RIGHT TIME.

If the firing isn't related to an egregious or dangerous act, plan the right day. Monday makes you a jerk. The next three days are odd numbers. Most employers think that Friday is best, but pick the day most suitable for your crew.

❷ SELECT YOUR TERRITORY.

The location should be private enough to allow the soon-to-be-dismissed employee some dignity but not so secluded as to allow any unforeseen negative consequences. Keep the environment simple and free of distractions. Do not answer phones or check e-mail during the termination.

❸ MAKE SURE YOU HAVE A WITNESS ON HAND.

In case it comes down to your word vs. the employee's, it is important to have someone else present. An HR staffer is most appropriate, but, failing that, pick someone reasonably neutral. The witness's role is to say little or nothing, simply to be there as an observant third party.

❹ KEEP IT BRIEF.

This is not the time for negotiation. If you have decided to fire an employee, state it very simply. "We're sorry, but this isn't going to work out. We're going to have to let you go, effective immediately. We have a few documents to share with you, and then we'll walk you out." Brevity helps.

ESSENTIAL ADVICE FOR FIRERS

✓ REMEMBER THAT FIRING SOMEONE, UNLESS YOU ARE DOING SO FOR A GLARING FAILURE OR ETHICAL LAPSE, IS A PROCESS, NOT A MOMENT.

Firing a staff member is all about defining absolutely the staff member's role before he or she begins employment in your company, documenting all communications and/or role changes, and being honest and open about existing problems.

✓ MAKE SURE TO HAVE PREVIOUSLY DOCUMENTED THE EMPLOYEE'S CURRENT ROLE.

This needs to be a very clear black-and-white document. If changes have occurred to his or her job description or role, add all details to the document, and have the employee sign it.

✓ IF IT IS CLEAR THE STAFF MEMBER IS NOT FOLLOWING THE ROLE OUTLINE OR JOB DESCRIPTION, MAKE SURE THAT ALL COMMUNICATIONS BETWEEN THE TWO OF YOU ARE DOCUMENTED AND AGREED UPON.

✓ IF THE POTENTIAL TERMINATION IS NOT THE RESULT OF LEGAL OR ETHICAL

LAPSES OR HONESTY ISSUES, IT SHOWS GOOD PROFESSIONAL PRACTICE TO THE OTHER STAFF TO OFFER INSIGHT INTO AND ADVICE ON HOW TO RECTIFY A PERFORMANCE ISSUE.

Again, document that you have offered support and ensure that the support you offer expects results within a fixed timeline.

✓ WHEN TERMINATING AN EMPLOYEE, PRESENT ALL THE COMMUNICATION RELATIVE TO THE STAFF MEMBER'S POOR PERFORMANCE AND SIMPLY ASK, "WHAT WOULD YOU EXPECT THAT I DO?"

With a clear, concise, and accurate recording of both parties' dialogues, it will be crystal clear that the employee has not met performance targets as defined before beginning the role. You will both agree that he or she cannot meet your expectations.

✓ THE RESULT WILL BE AN OPEN UNDERSTANDING FROM BOTH PARTIES THAT TERMINATION IS NECESSARY.

HOW TO DEAL WITH A COMPLAINER

Expert Adviser

Jon Gordon, www.jongordon.com

---

❶ SEND AN E-MAIL TO THE ENTIRE COMPANY ABOUT "THE HIGH COST OF COMPLAINING."

Tell your team that you welcome constructive criticisms, but that general complaints and negativity without potential solutions can have a huge negative impact on morale, productivity, performance, and success.

❷ INVOKE THE "NO COMPLAINING" RULE.

Inform all employees that it is prohibited to mindlessly complain to colleagues and/or team members. If staff members have a problem or complaint about their job, organization, customers, or anything else, they are encouraged to bring the issue to their manager or to someone in a position to address the problem. Explain, however, that they must also identify one or two possible solutions and share those as well.

ENCOURAGE JUSTIFIABLE COMPLAINING.

Discuss the difference between mindless complaining and justifiable complaining. Explain that mindless complaining focuses on problems, whereas justifiable complaining focuses on solutions.

4 IDENTIFY AND SHARE YOUR COMPLAINT PROCESS.

It is essential that each person in your organization understand how your company will consider and address complaints and turn problems into solutions. There are many possible options, and you must decide what works best for your type of organization.

5 LISTEN CAREFULLY AND ACT ACCORDINGLY.

For the "No Complaining" process to work, employees need to know that their justifiable complaints and solutions will be heard and considered. Their proposed solutions do not necessarily have to be acted upon, but staff will want to know that their ideas were considered. Therefore, it is essential that your organization address complaints, consider solutions, and act accordingly.

❻ CELEBRATE SUCCESS.

Shine a spotlight on those who have turned complaints into solutions and encourage and recognize those who have stopped complaining mindlessly to coworkers.

Be Aware

There is value in having a corporate culture that embraces constructive criticism and problem solving, so do not fear "complaints" per se. The key is channeling the energy towards fixing the priority problems and away from out and out griping.

HOW TO DEAL WITH NIGHTMARE EMPLOYEES

Expert Adviser
Roxanne Emmerich, www.thankgoditsmonday.com

✓ The Constant Bickerer

These usually come in pairs. Ask the most direct supervisor to meet with the bickerers to learn what it will take to eliminate the tension. Often just a conversation will do wonders. Secure a firm commitment on the part of both to improve. Spell out immediate consequences in case of failure.

✓ The Unclear Communicator

If you have employees with a pattern of saying, "But what I meant was . . . ," call them on it. Requiring the offender to have all communications checked for clarity for a certain period usually nips this problem in the bud.

✓ The Backstabber

This employee has a pattern of agreeing in public forums, but privately dissenting later. Make it clear that dissenting opinions are welcome during the decision making, but that once a decision is made, undercutting will not be tolerated.

✓ The Defender

Inform your staff that you consider a willingness to improve to be one of the hallmarks of a person with a bright future in the company. Defensiveness should be viewed as what it is: an unwillingness to improve oneself.

✓ The Chaos Creator

Pot stirring is a serious threat to productivity. Counter-balance the pleasure that the chaos creator gets from drama with a greater measure of negative consequences.

✓ The Incomplete Do-er

Let people know that they are expected to acknowledge errors and to make a commitment to clean up the mess.

✓ The Deflector

Deflecting blame equals deflecting responsibility. Make it clear that the only acceptable behavior is acceptance of responsibility and (as above) quick work to clean up the mess.

✓ The Pretender

This person is constantly claiming to have not received the e-mail, the memo, or the correct information. If there was no breakdown in the system, make it clear that the employee is responsible for consistently accessing internal communications—memos, e-mail, and so on—to ensure never again being out of the loop.

A NO COMPLAINT BOX *for potential solutions to problems—not just complaints—can reduce employee griping.*

✓ The Conflict Avoider

Conflict resolution is an essential part of a manager's job. The Conflict Avoider resists entering the fray of disputes. Performance reviews can and should count disruptive interpersonal conflicts against managers on whose watch they occur.

✓ The Gossiper

Once you establish a zero-tolerance policy for talking behind another person's back, give your staff permission to address conflict head-on, out loud, courageously, and honestly. And make it clear that giving or receiving gossip is unacceptable.

Be Aware

The dysfunctional workplace is a killer. Untreated, dysfunction will destroy your customer base, your profits, and your joy for living, as surely as anything.

HOW TO FEND OFF AN EMPLOYEE COUP

❶ DETERMINE THE LIKELY CAUSE(S) OF THE COUP.

The primary motivating factors are usually power (employees feel entitled to more), regime change (employees feel their leadership is failing), or disgruntlement (employees are feeling generally unhappy and abused).

The problem may also be a misunderstanding.

❷ BE OPEN TO THE POSSIBILITY THAT YOU WILL NEED TO CHANGE SOMETHING SIGNIFICANT IN YOUR ORGANIZATION TO RESOLVE THE SITUATION.

Do not simply assume that an attempted coup is a blatant grab for power. If significant problems did not exist with your company's morale, you would not be facing the situation (i.e., it would not have been possible to "rally" the troops to this cause).

❸ IDENTIFY THE LEADER OF THE ATTEMPTED MUTINY.

There is most likely one primary insubordinate whom you will have to deal with visibly and swiftly.

❹ DETERMINE THE NATURE OF THE LEADER'S MOTIVATION AND THE APPROPRIATENESS OF HIS OR HER ACTIONS.

Even if the leader is a valued employee who is motivated by factors that will benefit the company, if he or she has acted in a truly insubordinate manner, you will need to get rid of him or her. Moreover, if the leader is purely insubordinate and trying to protect him-/herself by enacting a coup, or trying to gain something from it, you should get rid of him or her. Be sure to make it clear (to both the leader and the staff) that the firing is due to a willful disobedience of orders, to undermining the company, and/or refusing to perform duties. Note that this does not necessarily mean you can dismiss the issues behind the attempted overthrow. Even a power-hungry coup leader can rally others to mutiny only if they are also feeling unhappy.

❺ ONCE YOU HAVE QUELLED THE INITIAL ATTEMPT, ENGAGE YOUR TEAM IN A MEANINGFUL PROCESS TO ADDRESS AND FIX THE ISSUES AT THE CORE OF THE COMPANY'S MORALE PROBLEM.

See the next scenario, "How to Restore Dangerously Low Morale."

Take your employees' anger seriously—there is most likely a legitimate reason for the mutiny.

❻ IF THE PROBLEM IS A CRISIS OF CONFIDENCE IN LEADERSHIP, YOU WILL NEED TO WORK TO GET BACK ON TRACK.

See "How to Fend Off Mission Drift," page 85.

❼ FIXING THIS SITUATION MUST BE YOUR FIRST PRIORITY—UNLESS THE SURVIVAL OF YOUR COMPANY IS AT STAKE.

If that is case, your company's survival is your first order of business. Give your team a "times are tough" pep talk (see the quotes on page 188 for reference). Promise that you will address their problems as soon as you make it through the storm. Then you can worry about low morale.

HOW TO RESTORE DANGEROUSLY LOW MORALE

Expert Advisers

Roxanne Emmerich, www.thankgoditsmonday.com

Lee Witt, www.brickhouseband.com

---

❶ ENGAGE IN A "STRENGTH BOMBARDMENT" EXERCISE.

Divide your team into groups of eight to ten. Invite everyone to sit in a circle and select one person to receive feedback. Proceed in order around the circle, with each person taking a turn and stating what he or she appreciates about that individual. When finished, select the next person as the feedback receiver and repeat until everyone in the circle has been bombarded with positive feedback appreciating their strengths. When the exercise is completed, everyone will feel extremely rewarded. People will never forget the day that the person they thought disliked them told them how much he or she respects them.

❷ GIVE YOUR EMPLOYEES A TITLE TO LIVE UP TO.

People do not just want something to do. They want to be someone. Give them a title. Make the person who handles incoming assignments and apportions them to the team the "chief of staff." Make the receptionist the "customer relations leader." Make your assistant the "executive navigator." Give them status and something to live up to, and things will start looking up.

❸ INVITE EVERYONE TO WRITE THEIR OWN MEANINGFUL VISION OR MISSION STATEMENT.

Announce that you recognize that the company vision and mission may leave some folks feeling a little cold. Allow staff to compose their own personal mission, stating whom they want to be, whom they want to serve, and what they want to accomplish. Then follow up by asking what it will feel like when they succeed.

❹ ASK STAFF WHAT WOULD MAKE THEM FEEL BETTER ABOUT THEIR SITUATION—AND THEN MAKE IT HAPPEN.

Set up one-on-one appointments and ask employees what it would take to improve morale. To the extent possible, implement what they tell you. The process itself will lift spirits, even before any changes are implemented.

Signs of dangerously low morale (excessive personal calls, drinking, slacking, crying) are not always this evident. Pay attention to your employees' moods and demeanors.

5 ESTABLISH INCENTIVES AND PERSONALIZE THE REWARD.

Your best performers want to feel that they are compensated accordingly. Establish bonuses for excellent productivity and be sure to personalize the reward. Give them the check in person, with your sincere thanks.

6 MAKE YOUR EMPLOYEES LOOK GOOD IN FRONT OF FAMILY MEMBERS.

Call the person's spouse and relate how much you appreciate your employee's contributions. Then thank the spouse for being so supportive of your employee.

7 EXAMINE YOUR OWN BEHAVIOR.

You may be the main reason that morale is low. If you are stressed, depressed, or frantic, your employees will sense it. Emotions are contagious. As a leader, you set the tone for your team. Be big enough to stay optimistic and energetic. They will pick up on that as well.

8 LIVE UP TO YOUR WORD.

If you say you are going to do something, do it. Always. If you make a mistake, apologize up-front. Trust takes years to build but a moment to lose.

 CLEAN UP YOUR MESSES.

Humans make mistakes, and if you're reading this, then you're human, so you will, too. But if you make a mistake or you're about to miss a deadline, own up to it immediately and clean up your mess. Let people know what an egregious error you have made. It is the best way to communicate that you care that you screwed up and are concerned about results.

Be Aware

You may have noticed a repeated refrain in this advice: Make it clear. Once you have determined to purge your workplace of dysfunctional behavior, your greatest ally and most powerful tool is clarity.

Basic Training

THE RULES

- Treat everyone with respect, no matter what.
- The ultimate form of respect is clarity—in both communication and expectations.
- "Respect" does not mean being a pushover.
- Put the important stuff in writing.
- Sweat the small stuff.
- Then again, don't sweat the small stuff.
- Counsel early and state clearly the consequences of failure.
- Never engage in gossip.
- You are not their friend. You are not their father. You are their boss.

TREAT EVERYONE WITH RESPECT, NO MATTER WHAT.

High school is over.

The days of proving how cool you are by cutting people down are long gone. Some employees may belittle others as a matter of course. They can get away with it. You can't. In fact, it is possible to be cool without cutting people down, and you'd do well to master the nuances of how it's done.

- Praise in public; criticize in private.
- Remember that a comment about a person may seem like a small thing, but it's often something that cuts to the very fiber of the recipient's being. ("Baldy" may be extremely self-conscious, even though you find humor in his lack of hair.)
- Some people make friends by hurtling insults at one another, but remember that not everyone can be so thick skinned. If you have a friend with whom you have such a rapport, remember to contain that behavior to that relationship and never carry it over to others.
- You can never go wrong by treating people respectfully—no matter what their station in life.

THE ULTIMATE FORM OF RESPECT IS CLARITY—IN BOTH COMMUNICATION AND EXPECTATIONS.

There is nothing more frustrating to an employee than a boss who loves the sound of his or her own voice.

Employees do not care how brilliant or witty you are. When it comes to you, they only care about what is expected of them and how well they are doing it. Blathering on is only going to make them fearful about their job (they do not know the criteria of a job well done), doubtful of your abilities (clear communication is the fundamental skill every leader must possess), and angry that their job sucks.

Think about it: If someone gives you unclear directions in an unfamiliar town, what do you do? The first thing you experience is confusion. Then you experience a little fear. Then you say to yourself, "What a schmuck," and then you seek out someone else for clearer instructions.

That is exactly what your employees do when you give them unclear instructions. The only difference is, the fear they experience is constant because at the end of the day you are still the person who signs their paychecks, and they worry they may still not be getting it right.

In fact, a lack of clarity can make people crazy. A study was conducted in which rats where confined to a cage with square sections. Some of the squares were electrified and emitted a little jolt. Here's the kicker: In one group, the squares that lit up were consistent. In the other group, the electrified squares changed randomly. Under the predictable conditions, the rats quickly adapted; they simply learned to avoid the electrified squares. In the setting with unpredictable conditions, however, the unfortunate rats quickly developed behaviors that resembled schizophrenia.

Do not make your team crazy.

"RESPECT" DOES NOT MEAN BEING A PUSHOVER.

Some bosses believe the way to win the respect of their team is to be nice.

In fact, the true path to earning respect is this: Be observed making decisions that are good for the company and that will help achieve your goals.

Sometimes employees ask for things that are detrimental to your objectives and to the rest of your team. Often they're not thinking about the far-reaching implications of their demands; they're thinking only of themselves. That's OK. It's not their job to think about the big picture. That's your job.

So, if you let their small-picture request damage the big picture because you want to be nice, it's not their fault. It's yours. They will respect you more if you do not let that happen.

⚠ PUT THE IMPORTANT STUFF IN WRITING.

This statement does not mean that every little event needs a contract or a record of the minutes.

What it means is that humans forget. You forget. Your team forgets. We all forget. So, put it in writing.

But remember, the writing is for both you and your team. It's for you to remember exactly what was agreed upon, and it's for your team to understand clearly what you expect. So, a single sheet of paper in your office filing cabinet is insufficient. What is needed is a clear system for recording exactly what was said and for passing on the message.

E-mail is a great tool for this purpose, but it can also become a huge productivity distraction. We recommend setting up unique e-mail accounts explicitly for business and ensuring that you cannot access nonbusiness messages when accessing work-related e-mails.

Alternatively, many effective and easy-to-use systems for delegating tasks exist online, such as www.simpleology.com, www.basecamphq.com, and www.clockingit.com.

SWEAT THE SMALL STUFF.

People remember when you remember their birthday.

It may be a small calendar entry for you, but for them it's a huge once-a-year event, one that is potentially wrapped in intense emotions. Birthdays can make people especially sensitive, and forgetting the date has been known to trigger some to contemplate or attempt suicide. If you're the only one to acknowledge the special day when all other friends and family have forgotten, your sensitivity is likely to engender great loyalty.

Keep a calendar noting important dates, anniversaries, and milestones and constantly scan a month ahead. Depending on the closeness of your relationships with your employees, you may decide to offer a bigger gift on a birthday or to mark a noteworthy milestone with a more obvious activity or celebration (e.g., sending an e-card on the twentieth anniversary of your loyal personal assistant's date of hire is likely to be perceived as somewhat inadequate).

Here are some important dates to remember:

• Birthdays (those of your team and their children)

• Anniversaries (only of their employment in your company; remembering your employees' wedding anniversaries is creepy)

• Holidays (make these occasions special for the whole team)

Sweating the small stuff also means that you need to recognize when people add special touches to their work. Don't worry about missing a minor detail here and there; it's impossible to always notice everything. Just make a mental note to point out exceptional work or behavior that you do notice and that is noteworthy.

Note: It's probably best not to comment on people's appearance unless doing so has professional significance. Noticing that an employee is wearing new shoes, a new hairstyle, or other physical change can easily be misunderstood.

⚠ THEN AGAIN, DON'T SWEAT THE SMALL STUFF.

Remember that everyone makes mistakes.

If someone on your team poured their heart into a report but you point out only that they forgot to dot an "i," you will likely engender their lasting hatred. Put yourself in your employees' shoes (hint: do so often), and you'll see what we mean.

View everything within the larger perspective of their

contribution to and the impact of the mistake. Then let the small stuff slide.

COUNSEL EARLY AND STATE CLEARLY THE CONSEQUENCES OF FAILURE.

When it's time to point out a mistake, don't allow the situation to fester. And use this moment sparingly. (Remember this quote: "Fire this weapon like a sniper, soldier: only when it matters and make it count.")

Telling someone what they did wrong two weeks ago is foolish for many reasons. First, they likely will have forgotten not only exactly what they did, but also the larger context of the questionable behavior. Second, it seems petty—and it is. Think of the message this approach sends to your team. ("My boss is not thinking about the big picture. He's obsessing about what I did two weeks ago.")

Now, when it's time to counsel someone, it is of supreme importance to let them know why. "Because it's the rule," is not enough. There is a reason for the rule, and if you can't communicate it clearly, you may want to question whether or not you should keep enforcing it.

Soldiers will flee a battlefield if they do not understand the aims of their government or if they do not believe in the cause. However, they often willingly lay down their lives for a greater purpose that they believe in and understand.

Similarly, when you explain to your team the reason for your seemingly arbitrary rule, you are far more likely to garner their support. Example: "Hey, Suzie needs you to fill out this form every day because she has to report it to the IRS or the company suffers a penalty."

⚠ NEVER ENGAGE IN GOSSIP.

A single comment from a leader can have far-reaching implications.

If a team member spreads a rumor, it is often easily forgotten. If you spread it, there is a ripple effect that will tear away at the very fabric of your company. Think of the unspoken messages you're sending to the person with whom you're gossiping:

a. You are a petty person (and they won't respect your leadership).

b. You cannot be told things in confidence because it may get around the office (and they will stop confiding in you).

c. You are constantly judging them (and they will be paranoid about making mistakes).

Just do not do it. If you do catch yourself gossiping, apologize immediately and carry on. And don't do it next time.

⚠ YOU ARE NOT THEIR FRIEND. YOU ARE NOT THEIR FATHER. YOU ARE THEIR BOSS.

It's lonely at the top.

That's one platitude with a whole lot of truth in it.

Yes, you can go out for a drink with your employees from time to time, but remember that they will not only remember how you behaved, they will also talk about it—to everyone.

If you are cool, kind, and in control, word will get around that you're easy-going (when appropriate) as well as a pillar of strength. If you get sloppy drunk (or emotional, petty, or angry), the fact that you behaved that way during "off time" will not help restore their loss of respect in you.

Chapter 3
Productivity Emergencies

HOW TO REMOVE PRODUCTIVITY LEECHES

Expert Adviser

Ryan Lee, www.ryanlee.com

---

❶ DO NOT CHECK YOUR E-MAIL FIRST THING IN THE DAY.

Check e-mail only after you've at least mapped out your priorities for the day, and ideally after you've worked at least an hour on the most important task you need to accomplish. E-mail will suck you into other issues you most likely do not need to deal with first thing in the workday.

❷ ELIMINATE INTERRUPTIONS.

Designate "project work time" during which, unless an emergency arises, you cannot be interrupted. Post a note on your door during these times.

❸ UNPLUG YOURSELF.

During your focused work time, turn off your cell phone, let calls go to voicemail, and turn off your e-mail and instant-messenger programs.

DON'TS	DOS
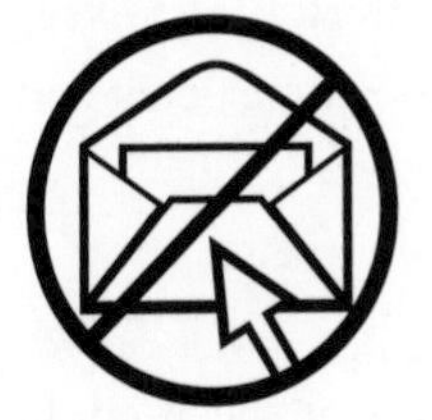 *Check e-mail first thing*	 *Eliminate interruptions*
 *Leave your cell on*	 *Break for sunshine*
	 *Work with a timer*

4 TAKE PRODUCTIVITY-ENHANCING BREAKS.

During your lunch, either hit the gym for a fast fifteen-minute workout or step outside and take a walk. These activities will recharge your batteries and keep you energized. Stay away from water-cooler chit-chat and bitch sessions with colleagues.

5 WORK WITH A TIMER.

Use a stopwatch and work in spurts of specified, focused time. Bursts of concentrated productivity have been shown to be extremely effective.

6 BLOCK DISTRACTING WEB SITES.

If you find yourself constantly checking your Facebook account during work time, run any of dozens of free software programs that block access to any site you desire.

7 PERFORM LIKE ACTIVITIES TOGETHER.

Block off thirty minutes to make all your phone calls. Block off another thirty minutes for answering e-mails. Such groupings are more productive than jumping from one task to another as they pop up.

HOW TO FEND OFF MISSION DRIFT

Expert Advisers

Spike Humer, www.spikehumer.com

Michael Fishman, www.michaelfishman.wordpress.com

---

1 REMEMBER THIS PHRASE: "VISION BEFORE MISSION."

Even a committed and passionate staff can lose sight and work astray of the company mission if it is not preceded by a well-conceived and articulated vision. The vision describes the company's larger purpose, perhaps even its global impact—by no means low-hanging fruit. The mission describes what the company does for its clients, employees, and stakeholders each day on the playing field. For true and lasting traction, a mission needs to exist in service of a vision.

Revisit the core purpose of your business and the reasons why you started the company in the first place. Ask yourself why it is important to you for the business to subsist, survive, and succeed. What is it that you and your company stand for? What are you trying to accomplish through your business, and why is that important to you?

❷ ALIGN (OR REALIGN) YOUR MISSION WITH A HIGHER PURPOSE.

Focus on who and what you are trying to serve. How will they benefit by and through your success, and why is it important to them? What do they lose if your mission isn't fulfilled? Why are they important to you, and how does their benefit serve you? What will you gain through the success of your business, and what would you lose if your mission is not pursued or continued? Rewrite and rearticulate your mission on paper.

❸ ENGAGE THE IDEAS, INPUT, SUPPORT, AND CONTRIBUTION OF THE KEY EMPLOYEES WHO ARE ESSENTIAL TO CARRYING OUT THE MISSION OF YOUR BUSINESS.

It is important to have the support of those most vital to the cause, but not at the expense of your own passion, values, and vision. Make the articulation of your mission as concise, tangible, and values-based as possible. Your mission must incorporate the values and principles most important to you.

❹ CUT OUT THE WEAK LINKS IN YOUR TEAM.

If you have contrarians running around impeding your organization's velocity and effectiveness, you must quickly and compassionately dismiss them. A mission that is closely managed will nearly always cause some associates to resign before their misfit becomes noticeable. Allow them to leave without protest from you; there is a reason they are opting out of the business. Better yet, be as rigorous as possible about hiring people who are a good fit for your culture and mission.

OUTLAW GOSSIP.

Gossip means talking to a listener(s) about a third absent person in such a way that the listener thinks less of that person. Praising someone in their absence is not gossip; it is praise. Gossip is a disabling virus, and if allowed to surface and run its natural course, it will derail an organization. If gossip begins, the listener should stop the speaker and request the presence of the third person so that the issue, complaint, or judgment can be aired and dealt with openly.

6 ENSURE THAT EVERYONE IN YOUR ORGANIZATION AND WITH WHOM YOU DO BUSINESS KNOWS THE REASON(S) FOR WHICH YOUR COMPANY EXISTS AND HOW IT RELATES TO OR SERVES THEM.

Encourage feedback about how you are living up to your mission and the values by which you want to run your company, and about what you want to be and whom you wish to benefit.

7 TRANSLATE YOUR MISSION INTO STRATEGY.

What are the best models, methods, and approaches to carry on your mission from today forward? What obstacles must you overcome or avoid? What strategies will give you the best leverage? How will they be implemented initially and supported on an ongoing basis?

8 TURN YOUR STRATEGY INTO TANGIBLE ACTIONS.

What actions, activities, decisions, and commitments must you make to ensure that your mission is ongoing? What organizational norms must you cultivate and reward? What policies, practices, and structures must you create and maintain to support your mission and its growth? How can these systems guide or direct your daily activities and decisions to ensure your greatest opportunity for success?

9 BE THE CHAMPION OF THE CAUSE.

Do not just think it. Do not just say it. Do not just have your mission written on a plaque on the wall. Live it, breathe it, "be" it. An effective mission statement should be compelling and propelling. Be a walking example and embodiment of your mission and the values it supports. Reward others for doing those things most consistent with your mission and demonstrating actions most consistent with the values most important and impactful to your business.

10 MEASURE YOUR PROGRESS.

Understand this: Where there is no profit, there is no mission in business. A mission cannot exist or be carried out unless supported by profit and profit-creating activities. Be strategic and pragmatic in your decision making in all possible things; measure results, activities, and decision effectiveness against your mission and your financial requirements to sustain your mission.

Make a pronounced commitment to your mission and the strategies that most support your values. In all major decisions or business matters, ask these questions:

If we are successful, does this action support or enhance the mission, vision, and values of the company?

Is there a more effective strategy, different decision, or alternative direction that will give us the results we want or need in our business and in support of our mission?

11 REDIRECT, REDEPLOY, OR REDESIGN.

Although a mission is not a destination, it is a way of being and a way of doing. If your activities, decisions, systems, or human resources are not aligned with your mission, it's time to make changes—not to the mission but to the organization.

Be Aware

Strength of purpose and commitment to a mission prevent mission drift. It is the regular practice and discipline to revisit, remember, and revive that strength of commitment that keeps you on track. With a strong enough why, the what to do and what not to do become easy and the how to do it becomes clear.

HOW TO FEND OFF "FEATURE CREEP"

Expert Adviser

Ric Thompson, www.smallbusinessceomagazine.com

---

❶ ASSEMBLE YOUR FULL TEAM AT THE BEGINNING OF THE PROJECT.

All too often, projects get expanded because a necessary participant joins the process late, coming in with a new perspective, desire, and need. Take the time before the project begins to ask, "Who else is needed here?"

❷ ASSESS WHETHER OR NOT YOUR TEAM IS TOO BIG.

To avoid "team bloating," decide if each and every person on the project team is truly needed. Remember, more people means more ideas, and though that can be great, there is a point of diminishing returns.

❸ MAKE SURE THE PROJECT'S OBJECTIVES ARE CLEAR.

Lack of clarity is frequently the biggest cause of feature creep. Make sure your goals and objectives are well established before you start developing the project. If your team is getting into the project and finding out things have not been fully thought out, more will have to be added during the development phase.

❹ MAP OUT EVERYTHING BEFORE YOU BEGIN.

Create mockups, flow charts, Venn diagrams—whatever is necessary to visualize the desired results. For example, if your project is Web based, have your Web designer create physical mockups of the final pages. Do not undertake any programming yet. First, look closely: You are looking at exactly what your customers would be looking at. What happens when users hit that button? What page are they directed to? What will happen behind the scenes? Do the mockups represent all possibilities? Is every function included? What's missing? Are there things that the customer would be looking for?

This step will not eliminate feature creep completely, but it will greatly reduce its likelihood and, more important, help you control it. You can use the mockups to determine if anything has been left out before full development gets under way.

❺ ASK EVERY STAKEHOLDER TO SIGN OFF ON THE PROJECT MOCKUPS.

In a perfect world, the mockups will be perfectly complete, represent every objective needed, and provide all the answers. In the real world, that is not going to happen. But if you make everyone involved sign off on the mockups, two things will happen:

People will look closely at them one last time to be sure not to miss anything before signing their name on the dotted line, thus hopefully catching major omissions or problems before development begins.

Although no one is perfect, some accountability must be assigned and accepted when failing to think things through. You will soon determine if any of your staff members fail in this regard and tend to add things later. After a few projects it will be obvious if the same person keeps overlooking major points and adding details. If that happens, assign another person to handle the planning portion, thereby making future projects flow a bit more smoothly.

Be Aware

"Feature creep" is the phenomenon that sometimes occurs when a project gets expanded too far beyond its original purpose, most often due to extra features that are added to it.

HOW TO FEND OFF DEATH BY MEETING

Expert Adviser

Dan Kuschell, www.dankuschell.com

---

❶ DO NOT HOLD REGULAR WEEKLY MEETINGS, UNLESS YOU HAVE A COMPELLING REASON TO DO SO.

You should not meet just because you always do at a certain time each week. Make sure you have a purpose and an outcome that you need to achieve.

❷ DO NOT HAVE A FULL-BLOWN MEETING WHEN A BRIEF PHONE CALL OR FACE-TO-FACE CONVERSATION WILL ACCOMPLISH THE SAME OBJECTIVE.

Even a well-crafted e-mail is better than a meeting if you are simply sharing information. You can solicit questions or follow-ups in your message.

PREPARE.

Set ground rules and outcomes for the meeting. Solicit input and feedback from other participants to determine their roles for the meeting. Do they have agenda items or will

It is the facilitator's job to keep the meeting on task and on time.

they simply be contributing listeners? Also, create an enjoyable environment. If you are providing food and drinks, prepare them ahead so that the meeting begins on time and stays on track. Have handouts, visuals, and equipment available before the meeting.

4. SET A REASONABLE START AND STOP TIME.
It is better to end a meeting early than to run long, so plan for more time than necessary. Aim to end your meetings five minutes early. Most people are used to meetings running long and will be pleasantly surprised if they get out early.

5. ASSIGN A FACILITATOR.
This person is responsible for keeping everything on track and on time.

6. START BY ANNOUNCING THE MEETING'S PURPOSE AND THE DESIRED OUTCOME.
Even if you have distributed the agenda beforehand, reiterating these points will either emphasize the purpose or introduce the ideas to new participants who have not had time to look things over. Use the agenda to stay on track.

7. ENCOURAGE PARTICIPATION.
Include everyone in the discussion. If participants are sitting silently, draw them out by asking directly for their input at key times. Recognize and appreciate everyone for their

contributions as they speak. Such recognition will encourage others to participate as well.

❽ RECORD THE MEETING.

Assign a note-taker to capture the main topics in writing; then distribute the notes for follow through.

❾ CLOSE WITH A SUMMARY OF THE FOCUSED ACTIONS TO BE TAKEN.

Identify the action items and the timeframe by which they must be accomplished. Prioritize them from most important to least important.

HOW TO IDENTIFY THE TRUE PRIORITIES

Expert Advisers

Andrew Miller, www.acmconsulting.ca

Lee Witt, www.brickhouseband.com

---

❶ STOP WHAT YOU ARE DOING.

Go to your office alone. Sit down. Shut off the phone. Be quiet. Breathe.

❷ VISIT THE BOTTOM LINE AND IDENTIFY THE TARGET OF YOUR BUSINESS.

Ask yourself, What is the true target of this business? What product really brings in the revenue, and who is the customer?

❸ GATHER KEY MEMBERS OF YOUR MANAGEMENT TEAM AND VERIFY YOUR ANSWERS.

Share your answers and see if your managers agree. Converse until you all agree upon the target of your business, that is, who you are serving and what is actually making you money. This is not about what everyone likes to do. It is about what you do that makes money for the business.

❹ GET EVERYTHING OUT OF THE TARGET'S WAY.

Once you agree, remove any activity that is not about the target. If what you are doing is not supporting your product and customer, why are you doing it? Identify the non–value-added activities and stop doing them.

❺ FOCUS ON YOUR TARGET AND EXECUTE.

Your priority is not your fancy new production machinery. It is not your nice clean new office. It is not your cool stationery and business cards. It is not phone calls, meetings, and continuous conversation about your product or service. Your target is to produce an outstanding product for a satisfied customer and then to collect the rewards. Do that and you'll stay in the phone book.

HOW TO RESUSCITATE INNOVATION

Expert Adviser

Caleb Jennings, www.calebjennings.com

---

❶ STEP BACK FROM THE DAY-TO-DAY TO DETERMINE WHERE INNOVATION IS STALLED AND WHY.

Determine whether one person or the whole team is causing the halt. Be honest with yourself in this audit—sometimes the one with the creative block is you. Putting some distance between you and the office will help you identify who or what really needs "creative CPR."

❷ DO SOMETHING WILD OR EXTREME TO INSPIRE NEW THINKING.

Neurological studies have shown that viewing a new and extravagant sight or experiencing an activity outside your comfort zone forces your brain to build new connections and reorganize at a higher level. By engaging yourself and/or your team in something as simple as a nature hike (or as extreme as skydiving), you will experience a significant boost in creativity and innovation.

 SEEK AN OUTSIDE OPINION.

Ask those outside your organization, whose opinion you respect, to share honestly what they see as being stressful or uncoordinated within your organization. Stress, whether obvious or subtle, is usually the main culprit in "innovation blocks" (as in writer's block or artist's block).

❹ INVITE A GUEST INNOVATOR TO SPEAK TO YOUR TEAM.

When an outside authority shares opinions on the subject at hand, something magical (and scientific) happens. Just as in a conversation with someone with whom you have a lot in common, your brain starts to make more and more connections to the knowledge you have stored in your head.

Inspiration + Linking Connections = Innovation!

As an added bonus, this exercise will also boost team morale.

❺ FIND MORE HEADS.

More heads are always better than one. If your team boasts only one innovator, you need more. Whether or not the additional person has any experience in what you do, a second mind focused on your project can help spark innovative thinking more than a single person is able to achieve alone.

6 TRY A BRAIN DUMP.

Try this exercise regularly by yourself and with your team. On a blank piece of paper or in a Word document, write at the top your name, the words Brain Dump, and the date and time. Just start writing. Anything. Seriously, write or type whatever comes to mind, whatever is bugging you, or whatever is repeating in your head. It could be song lyrics, things about your personal life, or any number of random things. The point is to clear your mind of thoughts that are impeding the progress of your creativity.

7 REENGAGE AND FOCUS IN SHORT SPURTS OF CREATIVITY.

After trying some or all of the exercises described above, meet with your team. Remove all distractions and focus on the project at hand for ninety-minute blocks, with fifteen-minute breaks between. This focus technique, mixed with the stimulation from any of the exercises you've completed, is a sure-fire recipe for "Resuscitating Innovation."

Basic Training

THE RULES

- Know what you're doing.
- If you can't describe what you're doing as a process, you don't know what you're doing.
- Use clearly measurable standards of quality.

  Note: The above rules can be summarized, "Know what, by whom, and how well."
- Once you have identified the process, consider scaling it.
- Know why you're doing it—and let your team know why.
- Recognize excellent performance, but only when truly excellent.
- Remove distractions.
- Do not harass or hound your team and then expect them to be productive.
- Remember that creative work does not follow your personal timetable.
- However, creative work without a clear timetable (or a clear goal) will not get done.

KNOW WHAT YOU'RE DOING.

This rule is glaringly obvious but, surprisingly, rarely followed.

Ask most companies what they "do," and you will almost always get a vague answer. Equally vague is the future prospect of such companies. This is important on both a macro and a micro level. Knowing clearly what you are doing day to day will radically boost productivity.

Productivity can be measured by your moment-to-moment actions. Time spent bumbling around figuring out what to do is time lost. And within organizations, a surprisingly large amount of time is spent in exactly this way.

Happily, however, such problems can be resolved immediately by considering the larger objective and then figuring out the next step. A great tool used by the U.S. Army is the backward planning method. Simply begin with the "desired end state" in mind and then project yourself into the future. Imagine you've achieved your desired goal. Then ask yourself what you did right before that. Then right before that. And so on.

IF YOU CAN'T DESCRIBE WHAT YOU'RE DOING AS A PROCESS, YOU DON'T KNOW WHAT YOU'RE DOING.

Businesses that are truly successful are not just successful once—they're successful again and again.

It takes many tries to get something right, so if your business is based on you creatively getting things right every day, your chances for success are exceedingly low.

The way to be successful regularly is to be successful systematically. The dishwasher in your kitchen doesn't come up with creative new ways to wash dishes each time. It follows a deliberate programmed process, and all you need to do is push a button for it to work.

Your business should operate in the same systematic way (without the detergent).

Even businesses that are based on regular creative output can be systematic. There are systematic ways to think creatively, and structures for good creative works. What's more, there are systematic ways to think of marketing your creative works as well.

So, how does one think systematically?

The best way is to map out what you're doing as a process. A "process map" is simply a visual representation of the steps required to perform a particular task. There are as many ways to map out processes as there are people, and the level of detail depends on the complexity of the task and the knowledge of the person doing the job.

The important thing is to just sit down and do it. Even if you're mapping out the process on a blank piece of paper in pencil, that's usually enough. Don't worry about having the perfect tool for getting the job done.

Once you have completed the process map, review it

with those who will be performing the job and be sure they understand it. Then make sure that when, in the future, other people do the same job, they use the same resource each and every time to ensure consistency of quality.

USE CLEARLY MEASURABLE STANDARDS OF QUALITY.

Once you have communicated what you want done, it is important that people have clear methods for understanding how well you want the job done.

Some things require great attention to quality standards. (A presentation to a key client, for example, requires a certain amount of tasteful polish.) Others do not need as much finesse. (A statistical reporting of facts does not need to be accompanied by an after-dinner mint.)

The way to communicate the level of accomplishment you seek is to accompany your process maps with a checklist. The checklist should include important "musts" that define your standards of quality. If you don't clearly communicate this aspect, expect your standards to be low most of the time and almost never what you expect.

⚠ ONCE YOU HAVE IDENTIFIED THE PROCESS, CONSIDER SCALING IT.

If your company's profitability can be measured by the output of certain key elements (i.e., increased production and an increased ability to sell what you produce), then "scaling" the output of these elements will increase your profitability.

If one person can create five bottles an hour, then two people can produce ten—but only if you have identified the key processes that make this happen.

Just remember that scaling pure production on its own is not enough. You must also scale your ability to sell what you produce.

If you can scale both of these things in unison, then you can also scale how much money you make, and that's a beautiful thing.

⚠ KNOW WHY YOU'RE DOING IT—AND LET YOUR TEAM KNOW WHY.

People need a purpose to feel fulfilled and happy.

If your employees are doing things mindlessly or without a purpose, the quality of their work will suffer dearly.

Imagine you are a cola bottling company. The people on the production line that makes the bottles may not realize that their bottles are shipped to all ends of the earth, bringing refreshment to people who need it. Encourage them to imagine the guy who has been working diligently all day and then cracks open a bottle of your beverage—and the joy and refreshment he feels in that moment.

This knowledge suddenly transforms the job of just "making bottles" into the job of "delivering refreshment."

That's a huge shift in perspective that will not only radically boost your production but also bring a great deal of happiness to what may have been a rather dreary job.

⚠ RECOGNIZE EXCELLENT PERFORMANCE, BUT ONLY WHEN TRULY EXCELLENT.

People like to be told that they are doing a good job. In fact, if you fail to recognize it, they'll think it's not important and will then stop doing it.

When someone does something exceptional, point it out—and do so publicly, but with the following provisos:

a. You run the risk of appearing to engage in favoritism, so make sure it's a fair comment that anyone else can achieve.

b. Only praise when something is genuinely worthy of praise. If you praise the silliest thing, people will feel manipulated and they'll be right.

c. Avoid constantly praising the same people while

neglecting others. It will make the others hate both you and the object of your praise.

⚠ REMOVE DISTRACTIONS.

Unless vital for the job at hand, shut off your cell phones, turn off your e-mail, close the doors, turn off the TV.

When it's work time, you should always have in front of you only what is essential to get the job done. Everything else is a distraction.

The problem with distraction is more far-reaching than you might realize. You may think a momentary distraction takes away only a few moments of your time. But in fact it can take away as much as fifteen minutes or more. If someone is engaged in creative work that requires deep thought, each momentary distraction also encompasses the time spent to reorient oneself to the problem.

If you have people in your office who need to be on the phone and e-mail all day, try to segregate them from those who do not need to engage in these activities.

Unless it is vital to keep up the pace of deal-flow, consider setting a policy whereby people check their e-mail only once or twice a day. Of course, once such a policy is established, don't then expect staff to have read an e-mail you sent thirty minutes ago.

⚠ DO NOT HARASS OR HOUND YOUR TEAM AND THEN EXPECT THEM TO BE PRODUCTIVE.

"OK, you're brilliant. You have lots of ideas. We get it. This doesn't mean you need to call me into your office every time you have a brainstorm."

If you need to talk to your team all the time, that only tells them how insecure you are—not how brilliant you are. State what you expect of them and then get out of their way. Check in from time to time and take corrective action when necessary, but other than that, leave them be.

⚠ REMEMBER THAT CREATIVE WORK DOES NOT FOLLOW YOUR PERSONAL TIMETABLE.

Works of creative genius cannot be produced on demand. The creative process is often a fickle one and largely performed unconsciously.

Sometimes ideas need to "incubate" in the mind before coming to fruition.

Also, if you try to treat your creative employees in the same manner as you deal with those on your production line, you'll likely be faced with a mutiny.

⚠ HOWEVER, CREATIVE WORK WITHOUT A CLEAR TIMETABLE (OR A CLEAR GOAL) WILL NOT GET DONE.

The paradox is obvious, but it is a reality we must face.

The converse to the rule above is that if you leave creative types to their own devices, without any pressure, they will likely "incubate" indefinitely.

Assign a deadline to your creatives, and hold them to it. However, do not micromanage their time in between. How they get the job done shouldn't matter to you as long as it gets done (even if their way of working requires 50 percent of their time at the foosball table and 50 percent doing the actual work).

Chapter 4
Sales and Marketing Emergencies

HOW TO CREATE A KILLER AD—YESTERDAY

Expert Advisers

Chris Brogan, www.chrisbrogan.com

Dr. Joe Vitale, www.joevitale.com

---

❶ REMEMBER THAT AN AD WITHOUT GRAPHICS WILL BE CHEAPER AND EASIER TO CREATE.

If your ad is text only, with carefully chosen words and a nice design, that's already a lot less work than a photograph or a graphic. Opt for a solid background, a crisp font, and a few words—tops.

❷ THINK OF YOUR CUSTOMER AS SOMEONE YOU KNOW INTIMATELY.

As David Ogilvy said, "The consumer is not a moron; she is your wife." Be brief and clear. In our culture of irony and snark, it would likely stun people to encounter an ad that is plain and honest.

❸ REMEMBER THE AIDA FORMULA: ATTENTION/INTEREST/DESIRE/ACTION.

First, a great ad grabs the reader's attention: *This Ad May Save Your Business*. Next, it must gain their interest: *There has never been a more difficult time for businesses to succeed. Thankfully, there has never been a better business resource than this one*. It should then spark some desire in the consumer to acquire the product or to learn more: *If you want to take steps to save your company, you must act now—today, not tomorrow*. Finally, it must give them a call to action. *Visit www.worstcasesbusiness.com today to stop the disaster before it kills your company.*

4 USE ONE OF THESE TRIED-AND-TRUE HEADLINES TO KICKSTART YOUR AD.

"Who wants ______?"
"Warning: Read this before ______."
"The shocking truth about ______."
"Give me 5 minutes and I'll show you ______."

5 CONSIDER RUNNING A SERIES OF THREE ADS IN A SINGLE PUBLICATION OR ON A WEB SITE, RATHER THAN JUST ONE.

Things fade from vision once they're familiar. Consider changing the text and/or the color and running the ad several times to hammer your message home.

HOW TO SALVAGE A FAILED MARKETING CAMPAIGN

Expert Adviser

Del Breckenfeld, www.officialcoolfactor.com

---

❶ ADMIT THAT THE CAMPAIGN IS NOT WORKING.

This is the first step on the road to recovery, but it is sometimes the most difficult; too many companies throw good money after bad trying to revive a campaign that might have been doomed from the start. Great leadership knows when to abandon an idea that is just not making the grade.

❷ REMEMBER THAT MARKETING BY COMMITTEE NEVER WORKS.

Egos must be set aside and your marketing team must concentrate on one solid idea—no one person is to blame and everyone will get credit when it succeeds. Human nature (particularly in the business world) is thinking your idea is the best without taking into consideration the overall theme or "hook." Every hit song has a hook—the part that sticks in the listener's mind. In a band, members can contribute, but if everyone forces in their favorite line or riff, they wouldn't have much of a listenable song, and certainly not a hit. Think of the hook as the one theme or point you want consumers to remember.

❸ REENERGIZE YOUR CAMPAIGN WITH A COOL PROPERTY OR A CELEBRITY.

Celebrities or famous songs have equity they can monetize, so it's worth every penny if your campaign can share some of that equity: coolness by association. With poorly planned models like the 1980s' Cimarron, GM diluted the Cadillac brand so much that it was close to extinction by early 2000. Brands like Lexus and Mercedes took its place as the baby boomer's status symbol. That all changed in 2003 when Cadillac unleashed the "Break Through" campaign during Super Bowl XXXVII. It featured a retro big-finned Caddy convertible from their glory years, backed by the soundtrack of Led Zeppelin's "Rock 'n' Roll." That ad got the viewer's pulse racing to the tune of an immediate 16 percent sales increase. The Caddy was back—in a big way.

❹ SUPPORT THE RELAUNCH 100 PERCENT.

It is crucial that you inspire the whole company, top to bottom, to get behind the campaign. This means that your Web initiative, sales team, and all collateral support from marketing services must hit the ground running in a unified effort. Once your campaign is reenergized, you will be surprised at how quickly that energy will transfer to your consumer.

5 LET GO OF THE OLD AND FOCUS ON THE NEW.

If a major campaign is failing, it is already under most consumers' radar. Once you have the major relaunch, particularly with a fresh, new, exciting hook, it will be as if the first campaign never existed.

HOW TO MARKET WITHOUT MONEY

Expert Advisers

Dan Kuschell, www.dankuschell.com
Ryan Lee, www.ryanlee.com
Andrew Lock, www.helpmybusiness.com
Dean Hunt, www.deanhunt.com
Corey Perlman, www.ebootcampbook.com

---

1 BECOME AN ATTENTION SEEKER.

If you lack a budget, you will need to stand out somehow from your competitors. This is not an additional extra; this is a must-have. Focus on a positive or negative from you or your service, product, or market and exaggerate it as much as possible. This is a quick way of ensuring that you stand out.

Remember that word-of-mouth is the most powerful form of marketing. If you can create a reason for people to talk about your products or services, the mouths will take it from there.

Also, try to do the opposite of what everyone else is doing—it is the easiest way to appear to be a creative genius. Grab a piece of paper. On the left side, write “always.” On the right side, write “never.” Fill in as many things as possible that someone in your industry never does and always does. Then pick one and do the opposite.

❷ POST COMMENTS ON BLOGS RELATED TO YOUR INDUSTRY.

This is a powerful strategy for enticing others to visit your Web site. Suppose you are in the business of selling collectible posters. Search for the phrase "collectible posters blog" to find blogs in your niche and then locate the most popular ones. Next, add an intelligent, helpful comment in response to a post. When you do, you will be invited to include your own site's URL. If your comment resonates with other visitors, they can click on your name and be taken directly to your own Web site to see what you have to offer on the subject.

❸ SUBMIT A WEEKLY PRESS RELEASE TO WWW.PRLOG.COM, A FREE SUBMISSION SERVICE THAT BROADCASTS YOUR PRESS RELEASE ALL OVER THE WEB.

The most effective press releases are those that either (a) are controversial, (b) tie in with topical news, or (c) arouse curiosity. The most common pitfall is that people write them like a sales letter. That type of press release will either be rejected or go completely unnoticed. Instead, make sure your text reads like a news story, something you would read in a newspaper. Make it factual and avoid hype. And, as always, be sure to include your Web site URL.

PROPOSE A JOINT-VENTURE PARTNERSHIP WITH OTHER COMPANIES IN YOUR NICHE, AND SPLIT THE PROFITS OF EACH SALE.

It is easy to find suitable candidates—simply search using keywords that relate to your industry and then look at the AdSense ads that appear on the right-hand side of the Web page. These ads prove that a company is willing to spend money promoting their product or service, so it will be easy to persuade them to try a method of making money that doesn't require them to spend more money. Ideally, you should call them with your proposal (that they offer your product to their customers, in return for a substantial share of the profits). Be friendly and emphasize the merits of your product or service.

5 POST CLASSIFIED ADS ON THE MANY ON-LINE CLASSIFIED-AD WEB SITES.

Keep your message brief and to the point, with a compelling reason for the prospect to respond. Also, provide multiple ways for people to respond, for example, via fax, phone, mail, or by visiting your Web site. These classified-ad postings will attract people to your site and provide you with many "backlinks" from these Web sites to yours, which will help raise the profile of your Web site on natural search-engine rankings. Sites that let you post classified ads for free include www.Craigslist.org as well as www.Kijiji.com, www.AmericanClassifieds.com, www.Loot.com,

Use the following tactics to market without money:

Start a blog

Write a press release

Seek a partnership

Place a free classified ad

www.Backpage.com, www.Gumtree.com, www.Oodle.com, www.Local.com, and www.Usfreeads.com.

6 START A BLOG THAT HELPS AND EDUCATES PEOPLE RATHER THAN TRIES TO SELL TO THEM.

You can set up a free blog using services such as www.SquareSpace.com or www.Weebly.com. Alternatively, choose a free Web hosting service such as www.Doteasy.com and install WordPress, which is also free. The most important point is to provide value to readers rather than trying to persuade them to buy. Offer value first, build a relationship with them so that they get to know, like, and trust you, and you will soon find that people will naturally ask what they can buy from you. This method of marketing takes time, but it is a solid approach to building a long-term business.

7 CREATE A FACEBOOK PAGE, A LINKEDIN PROFILE, AND A TWITTER ACCOUNT.

These are the largest social networking sites in the world and a great place to meet new people and find common interests. People who aggressively sell on these sites generally lose more than they gain by frustrating their audience and eventually alienating them as connections. When using these tools, be "human" and engage people in conversation. Just as at a face-to-face networking event, over time opportunities to work together could present themselves through uncovering common interests and the needs of others. The major difference between the two sites is that Facebook is much larger and tends to be more of a social site, where LinkedIn has a smaller community but the members tend to be more business focused.

Simply stating "what you're doing" won't get you far on Twitter unless your name is Ellen, Oprah, or CNN. Like Facebook and LinkedIn, it is about connecting with people and engaging in conversation. The more you interact with people, the more they will listen to what you have to say and suggest that others listen to you as well.

8 WRITE ONE ARTICLE PER MONTH.

Articles are similar to press releases, but your goal for the content should be to add value to your readers. Try using the "five tips" method. If you are a dentist, provide the "five tips to keeping your teeth healthy and white." If you are an online wine retailer, write an article about the "five tips to selecting great wines under $15." The more valuable the article, the more opportunity it has to spread—and that is free marketing. Once your article is written, you can add it to free article distribution sites on the Web (some are listed on page 121). Like press releases, articles can appear in search engines, so make sure you use those same keywords in your article.

9 CREATE A YOUTUBE VIDEO.

According to Alexa.com, YouTube.com is the third most popular site in the world, behind only Google and Yahoo. So, instead of trying to create the market, find out where they hang out and meet them there. Luckily, it has become amazingly easy to get videos about you or your business onto the Web. Digital cameras are perfectly affordable, and posting videos to YouTube is simple and free. Remember to always "hurl your URL" by ending each video with a way to get to your Web site.

10 OFFER TO HELP OTHER INFLUENTIAL BUSINESS OWNERS IN YOUR NICHE.

Not only will you develop valuable relationships with successful people, but a hidden marketing benefit will occur as well. When you help someone, you trigger a psychological rule called "reciprocity." In essence, it means that when you do something nice for another person, they cannot help but want to do something for you in return. You'll feel good about helping them, and they'll feel great about helping you back.

Be Aware

Marketing without money can actually produce better results than does throwing money around in "random acts of marketing."

HOW TO SELL WHEN NO ONE IS BUYING

Expert Adviser

Richard Webster, www.richardwebster.co.nz

---

❶ DO NOT GIVE UP.

Get used to rejection—embrace it as a part of the sales process, and keep up your calling. Designate a part of each day for cold calling. Eventually, you will find customers interested in what you have to sell.

❷ FOCUS ON MARKETING AND PUBLICITY.

If you can drive interest in and attention to your products or services, you can drive demand as well.

❸ COME UP WITH "AN OFFER YOU CAN'T REFUSE."

This does not mean a threat—some, but not most, people will buy out of fear—but rather a risk-free offer. Offer to place a display of your products with a retailer on consignment or extend payment terms that are too good to refuse. Offer to give a free seminar to the executives at a company you want to sell your services to. Offer free consultation services. Few companies will refuse a risk-free offer if they're at all interested in what you have to sell.

④ THINK LOCALLY, SELL GLOBALLY.

These days, you need not travel far and wide to find people connected to potential buyers for your services. Most likely, your friends and colleagues in your area as well as your database already have the leads you need to make sales happen. Reach out to your industry contacts and colleagues. Offer a commission for affiliate sales. Ask friends for help, and good things will happen.

HOW TO IDENTIFY A NIGHTMARE CUSTOMER

Expert Adviser

Dr. Debra Condren, www.businesspsychologysolutions.com

---

❶ REQUIRE PAYMENT FOR SERVICES AND PRODUCT UP-FRONT.

Include high-ticket items. Then do backflips through flaming hoops to overdeliver and make people feel that their money was well spent. This strategy also gets rid of so-called tire kickers who try to squeeze you for free advice or discounted services.

❷ MAKE IT EASY ON CLIENTS AND CUSTOMERS TO PAY BY SETTING UP A MERCHANT-SERVICES ACCOUNT WITH YOUR BANK SO THAT YOU CAN ACCEPT ALL MAJOR CREDIT CARDS.

Negotiate with your banking institution and shop around for the best percentage you are charged when accepting credit cards. Complete your application and have an account approved and ready to go within a few days to a couple weeks. When clients or customers book business over the phone, say, "My policy is payment in advance. Would you like to pay with credit card over the phone or mail me a check?" If they ask, "Do you ever make exceptions?" slightly restate what you just said. "I always follow my policy of requiring payment in advance to be fair to all my customers."

❸ CHARGE IN THE HIGH END OF YOUR INDUSTRY'S RANGE—EVEN IF YOUR BUSINESS IS NEW.

Do not undersell yourself. If you have extremely low rates compared with others in your industry, you are signaling to customers that your products and services are subpar. People who nickel and dime you and start complaining even before they have hired you are going to be pain-in-the-neck customers who are never satisfied. Pay attention and you will notice these and other early warning signs; when you do, don't hesitate. Say, "I don't think we're the right company for you to work with. Perhaps Acme Business down the road is a better fit." Sometimes this makes them want to work with you even more.

❹ UNDERPROMISE AND OVERDELIVER.

Practice excellent communication with your customers and clients. For example, studies show that the one key factor determining whether or not patients sue their physicians for malpractice has to do with bedside manner and doctor–patient communication skills: If a doctor has made an error, even one worthy of a malpractice complaint or lawsuit, but the patient feels that the physician has a track record of

HOW TO REPLACE YOUR NUMBER ONE CUSTOMER

1. **FIRST, TRY TO WIN BACK YOUR NUMBER ONE CUSTOMER.**
   Ask if there is anything you did that can be repaired or that you can do to improve. Do not beg or plead. Find out what it is that caused the fall-off in business and attempt to restore the situation. It can often be much easier to retrieve a customer or fix an ailing area of business than to find a new one.

2. **BEGIN TO ACTIVELY SEEK NEW CLIENTS.**
   Do not be afraid to go after "whales." If you do not seek them, you will never capture them.

3. **SEEK TO UPGRADE YOUR EXISTING B-LIST CLIENTS TO A-LIST BY SEEING IF YOU CAN IMPROVE YOUR LEVEL OF SERVICE.**
   Do not do so arbitrarily. If you can provide genuine added value, then make sure your customers know about it. If you cannot, do not simply ask them for more money or business.

SET UP A REFERRAL PROGRAM IN WHICH YOUR EXISTING CLIENTS BENEFIT BY BRINGING IN NEW CLIENTS.

Be sure their rewards are based on actual business (not just leads) and do not push it on them if it is not an easy yes. Being pushy makes them want to avoid doing business with you.

5 TRY, TRY AGAIN.

Keep at it. Eventually, you will find a new key customer. But if that does not happen quickly, be prepared to realign your business to the current realities of your income level.

Basic Training

THE RULES

- The core imperative of business is "Make an Offer."
- Prospects make their decisions with emotion and then justify them with logic.
- The purpose of marketing is to make selling easy (or obsolete).
- Do not be a salesman. Be a qualifier and a closer. (Match the right person with the right offer.)
- Branding and direct marketing are not mutually exclusive.
- Do not be afraid to sell.
- Assume the close.
- Never lie.
- Find (or create) a system that works.

THE CORE IMPERATIVE OF BUSINESS IS "MAKE AN OFFER."

Remember that any offer is an exchange. A quid pro quo. This for that.

At the heart of it, this point is what business is and all that business is.

You're asking the customer to part with their hard-earned money for something of value. Make sure that what you give them in exchange for what they are giving you is of equal (or, ideally, greater) value.

In sales and marketing, we are often told to "sell the sizzle and not the steak." Unfortunately, this has led to many businesses selling all sizzle and no steak.

The law has a name for this: scam.

Yes, people will get caught up in the drama and emotion of the sizzle, and that's a great way to stimulate the buying response. But if, after the sizzle, your customer does not bite into a piece of juicy steak that is not every bit as tasty as they imagined, they will experience buyer's remorse. In the best situation, this will lead to a refund. In a worst-case scenario, it will lead to them smearing you all across the Internet.

Put yourself in the shoes of your customer and imagine that you are experiencing what they experience. How will you feel at the end of it? If the answer is anything other than "ecstatic," go back to the drawing board.

PROSPECTS MAKE THEIR DECISIONS WITH EMOTION AND THEN JUSTIFY THEM WITH LOGIC.

This classic marketing truism is as old as the hills and equally dependable.

Buying decisions are an emotional process. Often people buy because of the mental projection of a future they perceive with your product that is tied to some deeper need. That's why you'll often see ads that show someone having a deep emotional experience while using a product. The advertiser hopes to link their product with those deep emotional images. This rule may seem incongruent with the above rule, but it's not.

It is perfectly OK to sell with emotion as long as at its core there is an offer that strongly benefits the consumer.

THE PURPOSE OF MARKETING IS TO MAKE SELLING EASY (OR OBSOLETE).

Your marketing is every bit about communication about your products, services, or company that your prospect experiences before the actual selling process takes place.

It is your branding, your advertising, your company image, the state of your bathrooms, the pictures on the side of your delivery vans, the word-of-mouth stories told about you in the marketplace—everything.

All of these aspects should be minded and managed such that by the time the selling process begins, the sale is easy. Or, better yet, already done.

⚠ DO NOT BE A SALESMAN. BE A QUALIFIER AND A CLOSER. (MATCH THE RIGHT PERSON WITH THE RIGHT OFFER.)

The selling of the past was often the hard sell. In this method, the salesperson assumed an adversarial relationship to the consumer and said "whatever must be said" to close the sale—even if it humiliated the customer or led to buyer's remorse.

This notion is antiquated. Modern salespeople understand that hard selling is not sustainable. Companies based on hard selling do not last long because either the marketplace will eat them alive (i.e., word about your practices will spread) or the consumer-protection agencies (both private and public) will.

The modern salesperson listens to the needs of the customer and matches them with the correct offer. Simply lead them to the right decision. If the right decision is to go with another firm, send them in that direction.

Really?

Yes, really.

Smart modern companies know that the world is too big to get too wrapped up about competition (with the rare exception of fiercely competitive markets with clearly limited prospects). The age of "co-opetition" is now.

Establish affiliate partnerships with competitors who

offer a different feature set and instruct your sales staff to send customers in that direction when you cannot satisfy them. You will then turn potentially lost sales into yet another revenue stream.

BRANDING AND DIRECT MARKETING ARE NOT MUTUALLY EXCLUSIVE.

When it comes to a measurable return on investment, nothing beats direct marketing.

Branding can be even more powerful, but the problem is that the impact of your efforts can be difficult to measure. As a result, many direct marketers say *branding* with the same disgust they reserve for a member of the Nazi party.

This is a mistake. Because you can (and should) embed branding messages into your direct marketing efforts.

In fact, if you can make every piece of advertising serve both branding and marketing purposes, you will be far ahead of 99 percent of the world's advertisers.

Make sure that each and every piece of marketing and advertising has the following:

a. A clear and consistent branding message about your product or company

b. A direct response mechanism (a URL, phone number, etc.)

c. An irresistible reason for people to contact you (the best reason is a freebie)

⚠ DO NOT BE AFRAID TO SELL.

Because of the unsavory tactics of the old-school hard-sell practitioners, selling has taken on a negative tone in modern culture. This is terribly unfortunate, because selling is a beautiful thing. When done properly, you are not taking people's money but solving people's problems. When you're selling within an ethical framework, the amount of money you earn becomes a measure not of how much you've robbed but of the good you've done.

⚠ ASSUME THE CLOSE.

The moment someone walks up to you (or calls or e-mails or whatever), assume they mean business. Chances are, they do.

A great example of how effective the "assumptive close" can be is displayed by the Girl Scouts. According to an old sales legend (probably unverifiable, but the lesson's validity is obvious), the Girl Scouts used to ask, "Would you like to buy some cookies today?" A clever marketer later advised them to revise it to: "How many boxes of cookies would you like?" And this minor change allegedly tripled their sales.

Again, the truth of this tale is unknown, but its effectiveness is irrefutable. Plus it illustrates beautifully not only how effective the assumptive close is, but how to do it.

NEVER LIE.

Ever.

FIND (OR CREATE) A SYSTEM THAT WORKS.

Creativity is a virtue, but not a good business plan. Sales and marketing processes should be reproduced—not re-created. Finding a correct sales and marketing process takes time. Once you find one, you should then think like a process manager and scale it. Scale means "cranking up production."

You can scale things in many ways. If your marketing is done by a person, engage more qualified people. If your marketing consists of ads on a Web site, get those ads on more Web sites. This simple fact is overlooked by most businesses, and that's why most businesses fail.

Some marketing processes, however, are not scalable—or are scalable only to a point.

If, for example, your marketing consists of you getting up on a stage, that process is scalable only by the number of speaking engagements you can handle. That is the limit of your company's growth.

But what if it's no longer you personally getting up on that stage, but people you train getting up on stage. Then your only limit is the number of people you can train and the number of stages you can find.

A scalable marketing process is one of the most powerful tools a business can discover. In fact, greatness almost requires it.

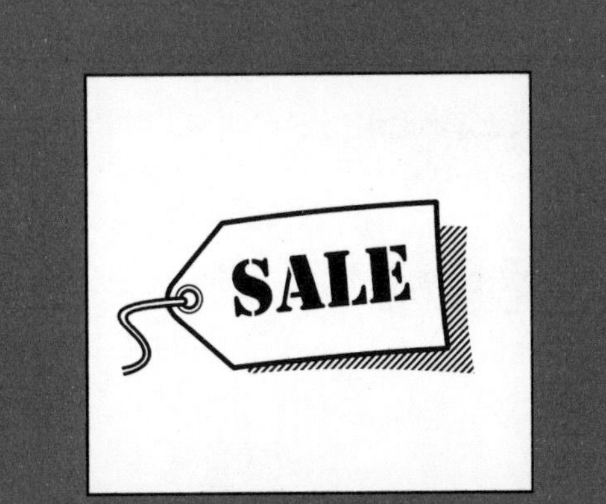
SALE

Chapter 5
Executive Emergencies

HOW TO ARTICULATE YOUR VISION

Expert Advisers

Dan Kuschell, www.dankuschell.com

Roxanne Emmerich, www.thankgoditsmonday.com

Joe Rubino, www.selfesteemsystem.com

OBTAIN ASSISTANCE FROM YOUR KEY EMPLOYEES.

You can get an immediate buy-in from your team by asking them to help you decide your organization's most important values. Start with examples of what the values could be and build upon that. Take the grand list and direct your team to identify the most important values. List them and distribute them to your staff.

2 PICTURE WHAT YOUR COMPANY WOULD LOOK LIKE, AND COULD ULTIMATELY BECOME, IF EVERYONE TRULY EMBODIED THOSE VALUES.

This will help you articulate a vision statement. For example, if you're a marketing and branding agency and you identify your core values as passion, creativity, responsibility, uniqueness, and ambition, you might come up with a vision statement such as: We are a marketing and branding firm that aims to create unique and distinctive campaigns for its clients, with passion, ambition, and responsibility of the owners of our client's companies.

3 KEEP IN MIND THAT A GREAT VISION STATEMENT IS SHORT, VISUAL, AND SERVICE ORIENTED.

Shorter is stronger. Examine any given sentence and ask which words are pulling their weight and which can take a hike. Change vague expressions such as "high-quality" and "world-class" into specific, powerful language that reflects your values. Simpler is also better. Use words that a fourth grader could understand.

Remember that there is a reason it's called a vision. A statement that fails to create a powerful visual image of the future is not a vision. It does not give people anything to keep in their mind's eye while they work. You need a landmark on the horizon or you're driving blind.

Make sure your vision statement reflects an intense, focused drive to serve the needs of your customers, not just to "satisfy."

BE BOLD.

The human spirit will not invest in mediocrity. That's why a vision always starts with a bold and audacious idea. A vision statement is nothing less than an invitation for others to invest in your dreams and a promise to do the same in return.

❺ COMMUNICATE YOUR VALUES AND VISION OFTEN.

Staff should see you and your management team leading by example, living and making decisions based on the company's values and vision.

❻ THEN COMMUNICATE THEM AGAIN AND REWARD THOSE WHO EXECUTE AND BEST EXEMPLIFY YOUR VALUES AND VISION.

Use a few minutes during regular staff meetings to reiterate the company's vision and values and to reward your staff for executing that vision. The passion with which you and your leadership team continuously reinforce the vision and values will determine how completely your vision is carried out.

❼ INSPECT WHAT YOU EXPECT, SO THEY HAVE RESPECT.

Many companies have a great concept of a vision; however, they tell staff members about it only once and then rely on them to remember it.

Joe Polish, one of the leading consultants in the world, says it this way: Tell them what you expect. Ultimately they will respect what you inspect.

Create an environment in which your staff and partners can take ownership in and of that vision. Make it a goal that they actively practice the organization's vision and values.

People are the key asset in any business. It should be

your goal to facilitate a culture that is customer, client, and staff driven.

Be Aware

- The vision and core values are the life of a business. They are much larger than a statement, a sign on a wall, or a saying.
- A company's vision and core values motivate and inspire staff and communicate to clients and vendors that your company is unique. They provide a common understanding of what the company stands for, a direction for where it is going, and, most important, an identity for what it is now and what it will be in the future.
- When an organization operates from its values and vision, leaders and staff alike will operate from that same set of values and vision in what they do and how they act.
- An organization's leadership is responsible for creating, building, and communicating the values and vision of that organization.
- A great leader takes steps to make that happen.

HOW TO DELIVER BAD NEWS

❶ BE EMOTIONALLY INTELLIGENT AS YOU CRAFT YOUR MESSAGE.

Put yourself in the place of those you are communicating with. How would you want to hear this news if you were them?

❷ TELL THEM IN PERSON; NOT BY E-MAIL.

Face-to-face is the best and most honorable way to deliver bad news. If you are far away, a phone call is acceptable (but still not as good as face-to-face communication).

❸ TELL THEM WHAT YOU ARE FEELING AND EXPERIENCING.

People need to know if you are suffering as well. Share your own emotions about the news you are delivering.

❹ LOOK FOR THE OPPORTUNITY WITHIN THE BAD NEWS AND SHARE THAT AS WELL, IF IT EXISTS.

Without putting a spin on the information you are delivering, share potential opportunities that may exist as a result. There is often a silver lining in any bad news.

DO NOT act or dress casually when delivering bad news. Do act solemn and serious—just not depressingly so.

SHARE WHATEVER NEXT STEPS ARE NECESSARY.

Once you have delivered the news, begin figuring out your next move. That might be a recovery or mitigation plan or just some form of additional support you can provide.

HOW TO APOLOGIZE TO ANYONE

Expert Adviser

Kevin Hogan, www.kevinhogan.com/worstcasescenario.htm

❶ DETERMINE WHAT YOUR LISTENER WANTS TO HEAR.

What do they think you did to them? How do they feel harmed? If they were 100 percent justified and you were in their shoes, what would you be feeling? Keep this in mind while deciding on your response.

❷ DETERMINE HOW LONG THEY HAVE FELT THIS WAY.

The longer the duration, the greater and more intense the resentment and anger they are holding in wait for you. Therefore, the greater the apology must be.

❸ DETERMINE IF A CORRECTION ABOVE AND BEYOND THE APOLOGY IS REQUIRED.

What else can you do to ameliorate, improve, or correct the situation? Can you offer free goods or services? Can you provide a refund? (If you do not know what you can offer, simply be prepared to ask, "What can I do for you to help you feel better about this?")

4 APOLOGIZE IN PERSON.

Face-to-face apologies are always better received. If you cannot do so in person, try to apologize with a phone call rather than an e-mail or letter.

5 APOLOGIZE SIMPLY AND SINCERELY.

You might say, "I feel very bad about what I did. It was a bad decision. I know this hurt you and I really screwed up. I can't make up for what happened, and I take full responsibility. I know it won't make up for this, but I'd appreciate it if you accepted X (a bonus, an incentive, a month of free parking) as a small gesture for the frustration you feel. I can only imagine how angry you must feel and how much you must resent what happened. It won't happen again."

"Now, I need you to tell me . . . when people do stupid things they often don't see everything they did wrong. Is there anything else I should know about this situation, because I need to make it right between us."

6 LISTEN.

Do not make excuses or offer an explanation for your actions unless asked. Do not offer to give a reason. Ask, "What else?"

 APOLOGIZE AGAIN.

They have now heard you apologize once. Apologize again, right now. When you are done, offer a handshake. "I can't change what I did. I can't change how you feel. But I can promise to do better from here on out. I hope you will forgive me."

HOW TO AVOID GETTING A DIVORCE

Expert Adviser

Kevin Hogan, www.kevinhogan.com/worstcasescenario.htm

---

❶ GATHER YOUR SPOUSE (OR YOUR ENTIRE FAMILY) INTO THE ROOM.

Turn off the computer and anything that could bring a distraction to this moment, including taking the telephone off the hook.

❷ SAY SOMETHING LIKE, "I WANT YOU TO KNOW THAT I HAVE COME TO REALIZE THAT I TREATED YOU NOT EVEN HALF AS GOOD AS I'VE TREATED THE PEOPLE WHO WORK FOR ME. AND WHEN I THINK ABOUT THAT, IT DEVASTATES ME."

Continue with, "I love you. The most important thing to me in the world, the reason I work as hard as I do, is so that we can have a secure home and family. But we haven't had a stable atmosphere, and I'm going to fix that. I need you to tell me what you would like me to do concerning work and our life together, which is obviously why I work as I do. I don't want you to hold anything back. Tell me everything.

Nothing is more important than us. I don't 'love' anyone at the office. I love you. And I need your help to understand what you expect of me. So, please, tell me what you would like me to do."

❸ SHUT UP AND LISTEN.

You have now shown more insight and awareness in thirty seconds than you have in years. Let the other person speak.

❹ WHEN YOUR FAMILY TELLS YOU THAT YOU CAN'T WORK AT HOME AT ALL BECAUSE IT STRESSES THEM OUT, ASK IF THEY WOULD PREFER YOU TO LEAVE WORK AT THE OFFICE, AND DO THAT.

As the executive, you don't earn a $50,000 salary. You earn $200,000 because you do the work of four people. And if being at the office instead of being around the house is what they prefer, do it.

❺ IF THEY WANT YOU AT HOME BUT WANT TO SPEND MORE TIME WITH YOU, DO THAT.

In most people's minds, Time = Love.

❻ BEGIN PERFORMING INTENTIONAL RANDOM ACTS OF KINDNESS EVERY DAY.

Bring home her favorite flowers . . . not just roses. Take your family out to dinner. Do something around the house you

Balancing work and family can be tricky.
When you are with your family, be *with your family.*

normally don't do, like helping to clean, in a way that prompts them to tell their friends, "He's really trying."

7 BEFORE TENSIONS WORSEN, OFFER TO SEE A COUNSELOR BY YOURSELF, AS A COUPLE, OR AS A FAMILY.

8 IF THE THREAT OF DIVORCE HAS BEEN PUT ON THE TABLE, REALIZE THAT IT IS REAL AND THAT YOU HAVE A PROBLEM THAT IS BIGGER THAN ANY PROBLEM AT WORK.

Treat the situation as you would a crisis at the office . . . times ten.

HOW TO DEAL WITH A SEVERE BRAIN FOG (AKA LACK OF FOCUS)

1. GET AWAY FROM YOUR DESK.

   Take a mini-vacation. Get some fresh air, go for a walk, or get some coffee. Clear your mind.

2. STOP AND BRING YOURSELF TO THE PRESENT MOMENT.

   Think about the one thing that has to be done right now. If the priority isn't clear, choose one. There may be thirty other things behind that one task that also need attention, but for now, those can wait. Stop ruminating on all the things you have to get done. Get clear on one thing to focus on.

3. EXECUTE THAT ONE THING.

   Do that one thing until it is complete.

4. SELECT THE NEXT THING TO BE DONE AND REPEAT STEPS 2 AND 3.

If you find that you are experiencing a brain fog,
get away from your office to clear your head.

❺ REMEMBER THAT YOU CAN ONLY WORK IN THE NOW.

It does not help to think about all that you have to do tomorrow or all that you should have done yesterday. Right now is when you can achieve something. Use this moment to move forward.

SHORT BUT SWEET SCENARIOS

The three short but sweet scenarios that follow are key to becoming an effective executive in a time of crisis.

HOW TO IDENTIFY AND FIX A FLAWED BUSINESS MODEL

1. **Begin by outlining your current business model.**

If you cannot write it on a cocktail napkin, it's probably too complex.

2. **Define "what you do."**

3. **Define your growth strategy. (See the "Basic Training" on page 163.)**

4. **Scale your business constantly, based on your growth strategy.**

5. **Do not deviate from your strategy.**

Trying to be everything to everyone is almost always the death of business.

HOW TO MAKE DIFFICULT DECISIONS

1. **Remember that "paralysis by analysis" is one of the primary killers of all businesses.**

2. **Remember that you will never know unless you try.**

3. **Stop debating, and take action.**

You will not know whether or not your decision was a bad one unless you give it a shot.

4. **Move ahead.**

HOW TO REGAIN THE RESPECT OF YOUR STAFF

1. **Be honest with them.**

Admit mistakes you have made, if warranted.

2. **Let them know that you are sincere about changing your relationship, and ask them individually to give you feedback on what you can improve.**

Do not open the floor to a group "let's fix the boss" session. Your staff will eviscerate you and will stop feeling responsible for their own actions.

3. **Send an e-mail to the entire group informing them that you have taken their feedback on board and are ready to start fresh.**

Communicate that you are sincerely grateful for the second chance and all their insightful comments. You might say, "I was especially appreciative of all the support you gave me in your messages."

4. **Act "as if."**

Do not walk around thinking paranoid thoughts. Act as if things are now better. Act as if they respect you. Treat them with respect. Be firm but fair. Know what you want them to do and expect them to do it. And remember that you are not their friend; you are their boss. Over time, that will become the reality.

Basic Training

THE RULES

- Have a clear vision.
- Clearly communicate your vision.
- Be an example.
- Avoid paralysis by analysis.
- Empower your team
- The only way to protect your intellectual property is through speed.
- Put on your own oxygen mask first.

HAVE A CLEAR VISION.

A leader without a direction will take his troops there: to an unknown destination.

For your business, that could be Wall Street or the poorhouse—and, without a direction, more likely the latter.

Your vision must be realized on both a macro and a micro level. A good place to start is here:

a. Your mission: What you want to do in the world on a grand scale

b. Your culture: How you treat people—both within and outside your company

c. Your goals: What specifically you want to accomplish in the next six months to a year

d. Your plan: What you are going to do today to make the above a reality

Is it really that simple?

Yes. And veering away from that simplicity is exactly how companies go wrong.

CLEARLY COMMUNICATE YOUR VISION.

If your vision remains in your head, there is one very important place it will not be: in the minds of your team.

Clearly communicate that vision to everyone necessary. Make it unwavering. Verify that your team not only understands it but lives it.

BE AN EXAMPLE.

If you can't follow your own standards, reset your standards.

"Do as I say not as I do" may excuse your incongruence in your own mind, but not in the minds of your team members. If that's how you live, they are far more likely to follow what you do than what you say.

AVOID PARALYSIS BY ANALYSIS.

There's one thing you're not doing when you're thinking: acting.

Thinking is extremely important, but it's easy to analyze a problem to death and suck the momentum out of your projects. A good way to think about it is to simply imagine the profit you make from even poor decisions.

If you make $10 from a poor decision, you might compare that to the $1,000 you could have made from the home run. Don't let that concern you. Simply compare it to the $0 you would have made from inaction. Over time, the quality of your decisions will improve and so will your profits.

EMPOWER YOUR TEAM.

Your team is probably smarter than you think.

If you follow the other rules set out in this book, you're likely to have a team that is loyal and happy. Communicate large outcomes to them and empower them to do whatever it takes to make it happen.

Warning: If they get the job done but are not 100 percent on the target you had in mind, you may be tempted to nitpick them to death until it becomes like the picture you have in your mind. News flash: It's never going to be exactly like the picture you have in your mind. You have to ask yourself what's more important: closeness to your mental picture or profitability?

You know the answer.

⚠ THE ONLY WAY TO PROTECT YOUR INTELLECTUAL PROPERTY IS THROUGH SPEED.

Yes, patents and copyright are important, but here's what no one tells you: enforcing them often takes more time and energy than any financial reward merits. It's extremely challenging to obtain a legal judgment in such cases. And collecting on the judgment is even more difficult.

So, attempting to fight such battles is really a losing proposition and should only be undertaken in the most egregious cases and when the defendant will likely be compelled to make restitution.

But 99.99 percent of the time, forget about all that.

Accept that your ideas, and often your work, will be ripped off. Beat them to it by coming to market harder and faster.

If you must go the legal route, put it in the hands of the toughest lawyer you can find (who bills fairly) and let them loose. Then forget about it.

⚠ PUT ON YOUR OWN OXYGEN MASK FIRST.

Your personal health and performance are far more important than most business owners realize. If you're healthier, the quality and quantity of your work will be much greater.

Moreover, a fit boss will naturally get far more respect than one who is obese, out of shape, slovenly, or otherwise unconcerned about personal health.

Take the job of taking care of yourself just as seriously as the job of taking care of your business. They are in fact one and the same.

How? Get enough rest (both sleep and "chill time" to relax your mind), drink sufficient water, minimize sugar and alcohol consumption, eat more vegetables. The key is to establish healthful habits that have life-long impact.

• Make a habit of getting a full night's sleep every night. Coming in late is better than coming in brain-dead.

• Drink a glass of water before every meal.

• Walk to places and take the stairs whenever you can.

These tiny habits will pay off huge dividends throughout your life.

Epilogue

"Get Your Mind Right"

Mark Joyner

Every business that ever existed—well, everything invented by humanity, for that matter—began as an idea in someone's mind.

To say this is one thing. To understand on a deep level the type of thinking required to convert ideas into reality is quite another.

Business is essentially the turning of ideas into things—and turning those things into money. That's a tremendously beautiful thing if you think about it. So, how does that happen? Well, there is in fact an ideal mindset for business success. This mindset may be the single most important thing that determines whether or not your business will succeed.

The ten ideas described below are what I use to teach my coaching clients this ideal mindset. You may resist some of them, but just try believing them for thirty days and see what happens.

❶ CHANGE IS POSSIBLE.

It is often said that "people never change." As is often the case with many things often said, that notion is utter and absolute rubbish. Having grown up in the poorest of families in the direst of circumstances and later becoming a philanthropist, a best-selling author with translations in twenty languages, an inventor, a decorated military officer, and an international figure, I stand before you as proof that change is possible. Not only is it possible, it's inevitable. As was said so well by George Malley in the film *Phenomenon*, "Everyone and everything is on its way to somewhere."

Perhaps a more important realization is that not only is change possible, conscious change is possible. Anyone, at any point in life, can change circumstances at will if desired. If you're not happy with your life, you have the power to change it anytime you choose.

Again, to understand this concept is one thing. To act on it, quite another. This leads us nicely to the next realization.

❷ YOU ARE RESPONSIBLE FOR YOUR OWN LIFE; NO ONE ELSE IS.

Stop blaming your circumstances. Stop blaming your parents. Stop blaming your past. Every moment of your life can be a conscious choice. Why not choose the things you truly want and refuse to settle for anything else?

❸ YOUR MOOD, YOUR PERSONALITY, AND YOUR ATTITUDE ARE A CHOICE.

Not only can you choose to have the things you really want, you can also choose how you feel and how you conduct yourself in the world. There are thousands of things (physical and psychological) to change your mood without taking Prozac. Most of the pain and suffering we experience is by choice as well. If you don't believe it, pay attention for a few days to how much of your suffering is actual experience and how much is you spending time imagining how terrible experiences have been or will be. Unless you're seriously ill, you'll likely find that about 99 percent of your suffering is all in your imagination.

❹ CHOOSING A GOOD MOOD, A POSITIVE ATTITUDE, AND A POWERFUL PERSONALITY WILL PAY OFF UNTOLD DIVIDENDS IN YOUR LIFE.

Not only will making this choice change the very nature of the way you experience your life, it will also open windows of opportunity that are closed to those who choose negativity and suffering. People will be more eager to work with you and spend time with you. You will give yourself more chances to succeed. Your whole world will be brighter.

Some may dismiss this advice with sarcasm. Look at them closely and see how that's working out for them.

❺ YOU MUST MERCILESSLY ROOT OUT ALL NEGATIVE PERSONALITY TRAITS (FRUSTRATION, GOSSIP, JEALOUSY, ANGER, AND SO ON).

Once you realize that a positive disposition is the key that unlocks a world of wonder, you must then mercilessly eliminate the habits of your old self that caused you to suffer. The habit of suffering begins in the small things. When you speak ill of others . . . When you choose to wallow in frustration . . . When you allow yourself to indulge in anger . . . These choices build up into a force of habit that consumes your better self. Instead, make a habit of being your better self by constantly reinforcing it through your daily actions.

❻ TRUST IN THE POWER OF YOUR OWN MIND.

Much of the power in the world is transferred in the ultimate confidence game. More often than not, it is not those who know better that rule the world, but those who convince others they do. Those who understand this dynamic often abuse it by brow-beating others into going along with their way of thinking.

The antidote is to respect your own thoughts. People often stifle the desire to express themselves, for fear of looking foolish. That is nothing less than an act of partial suicide. When you tell your mind that you don't trust it, it begins to shut down. The more you trust your own thoughts and ideas, the stronger your mind becomes.

❼ TRUST IN THE POWER OF YOUR OWN SENSES.

It is indeed true that our senses deceive us at times; but more often than not, they don't. The problem is not in our senses deceiving us, but in us deceiving ourselves about what it is that we see.

❽ KNOW WHAT YOU KNOW; DON'T KNOW WHAT YOU DON'T KNOW.

One of the worst habits nearly everyone develops is that of pretending to know something when we don't. The irony is that it's this very pretense that perpetuates the ignorance we're trying to hide. Develop the habit of asking questions when you don't know something. Some will ridicule you for not knowing, but you can amuse yourself with the knowledge that in time you will likely know far more than they do through your newfound habit.

❾ IT IS BETTER TO BE IRRATIONALLY OPTIMISTIC THAN IRRATIONALLY PESSIMISTIC.

Whatever the limits to human potential, they are likely far beyond what any of us has imagined. But imagine we can know this limit. If you are irrationally pessimistic, you will prevent yourself from experiencing this full limit. If you are irrationally optimistic, you will overshoot your limit and thus achieve your full potential. If that's too abstract, let's put it in terms of money. If your potential is to be a millionaire, but through your irrational pessimism you believe you're only capable of living in a slum, you will indeed forever live in a slum. If through irrational optimism you believe you can become a billionaire but only end up as a millionaire, well, you're still a millionaire.

⑩ THIS IS YOUR LIFE, NO ONE ELSE'S.

The grand tragicomic irony of most lives is that they are lived for other people. Even more ironic is that these other people for whom we are living are usually not around. It's the radical choice we didn't make for fear of what our parents might think. It's the career we didn't pursue because our teachers would not approve. It's every damn thing we do that slowly snuffs out our spirit, and for what? For whom? Whoever they are, they probably don't care, and if they do, they'll get over it. As Natasha Bedingfield said, "No one else can feel the rain on your skin. No one else can speak the words on your lips. Drench yourself in words unspoken. Live your life with arms wide open. Today is where your book begins. The rest is still unwritten."

Appendix

THE "YOU'RE FIRED" SPEECH

[*State person's name*], this is going to be a tough conversation. I'm sorry to tell you that I'm letting you go/terminating your employment/dismissing you, effective today. I know you're aware that we've had difficulties with you for a while and I had hoped that the probationary period and growth plan we mapped out in [*state timeframe*] would work. [*Or, if due to a major error or ethical lapse*: I'm sure you can guess why this is happening—this is specifically because of *(state incident)*].

This is a termination for cause. [*Optional:* However, I would like to offer you the opportunity to resign instead of being terminated.] It's clear to me that because [*state reason for termination, i.e.,* you have consistently failed to achieve your goals/you demonstrate a lack of ethics that I find unacceptable in an employee/you are simply not well suited to your position and are not performing at the high level we expect], you are no longer a good fit for the company.

[*Optional:* This is difficult for me as well, since I like you personally very much, and I wish that things were different. But it's clear to me that this has to happen.]

This is effective immediately. I am offering you [*describe severance*] *OR* I am not offering you severance. In order to receive it, you will need to return to us the [*separation agreement*] I am handing you, along with the full status memo that it describes. You can take [*state time-frame*] to review it.

I'm going to escort you to your desk to get your coat and any personal items you need right now; then we will set a time that's comfortable for you to come back, pack up, and say goodbye. I plan to gather the staff once you've left and tell them what has happened. I'm sorry that it has come to this, and I wish you the best of luck. [*shake hands*]

ANNOUNCING A TERMINATION TO YOUR STAFF

I wanted to get everyone together to let you know that a few minutes ago I had to do a difficult thing—I fired [*state employee's name*]. This was a termination for cause. [*State cause, i.e.,* She has been consistently missing her goals/She demonstrated a lack of ethics/She showed me over the past several months that she's not a good fit with our company]

[*Alternative version:* I wanted to get everyone together to let you know that (*state employee's name*) tendered her resignation today. She has decided that she is no longer a good fit with our company and would like to pursue other opportunities.]

This is effective immediately, and I told her that she would be able to set a time later this week to come back, pack up, and say her goodbyes. She received a fair severance package and understood the reasons behind the dismissal. I wish I didn't have to do this, but I had no choice. We deserve to have employees and coworkers who operate at the high level of performance at which you're all operating, and when I see such a glaring lack of performance I have to act, for everyone's sake.

We will discuss the plans for a replacement and the transition period over the next few days, and I'll let you know what that plan is.

I know this may be a surprise to some of you, and I know it's always sad to see a good friend and colleague leave, but I want you to know that there was ample opportunity for her to turn things around, and this firing had to take place for our greater good.

If you have any questions or things you'd like to discuss, my door is open. Thanks, and let's get back to work.

THE LAYOFF SPEECH

[*State person's name*], this is going to be a tough conversation. I'm sorry to tell you that due to economic conditions/a company-wide reorganization/a job restructuring, we are eliminating your position and I am letting you go today.

I'm sure you know [*describe the big picture here, i.e.,* we've had huge losses, and we have to cut our overhead by 10 percent in order to survive]. But it's always a surprise, and I'm sure this won't be easy.

I want you to know I looked at all other available alternatives before taking this course of action, but ultimately we had to look at what positions could most easily be eliminated/restructured, and unfortunately yours is one of them. I am also letting [*state additional names*] go today as well.

This is difficult for me as well, since I like you personally very much, and I wish that things were different. But it's clear to me that this has to happen.

This is effective immediately—I am offering you [*describe severance*]. In order to receive it, you will need to return to us the [*separation agreement*] I am handing you, along with the full status memo that it describes. You can take [*state timeframe*] to review it. I would also be happy to give you a good letter of recommendation and serve as a reference for you as you look for future employment.

I'm going to escort you to your desk to get your coat and any personal items you need right now; then we'll set a time that's comfortable for you to come back, pack up, and say goodbye. I plan to gather the staff once you've left and tell them what has happened. I'm sorry that it has come to this, and I wish you the best of luck. [*shake hands*]

THE "WE CAN'T PAY YOU ON TIME" SPEECH/E-MAIL

I wanted to give you a call to let you know that we aren't going to be able to pay our bill this month. Cash flow is tighter than expected, and rather than simply lie or stall I wanted to call to let you know personally, because we value your services immensely and I'd want the same treatment from you if you had a delivery issue. I hope you can understand and respect that. We will be able to pay you [*describe payment plan*] and expect to be back on track after that. But I'll stay in close touch and let you know if anything changes or if we can accelerate payment. Thanks for your understanding, and if you have any questions or concerns, do not hesitate to call.

THE ALL-PURPOSE APOLOGY

I wanted to call/e-mail because of [*state incident*]. I'm sorry that I made a mistake/screwed up/made a bad call. I want to apologize for my actions/poor word choice/bad decision. I don't really have any excuses except to say that I made a mistake, I'm truly sorry, and I accept full responsibility for my error. I don't want to try to justify myself or explain my choices—just to say that I'm sorry. I've learned a valuable business lesson. I hope you can respect and understand that, and that we can move on in the knowledge that I won't let this happen again. Is there anything I can do to help make up for this?

THE BREAKUP/"IT'S NOT YOU, IT'S ME" SPEECH FOR BUSINESS RELATIONSHIPS

We've worked together for a long time—[*state length of time*]—and it's been an amazing run. [*State accomplishments and history.*] We wouldn't be where we are without you, and I hope you feel the same way. But we're now a different kind of company than we were [*state number*] years ago, and our goals and needs have changed significantly. As a result, I've decided that we need to explore other options for [*state service*], and I wanted to let you know that as of today I am officially giving you notice that we intend to terminate our relationship as of [*state date*]. It's not that we're unhappy with anything on your end—to be sure, every relationship has issues. It's not like there's something you need to change in order to keep us. Our needs are simply different now, and we need to head off in new directions. I hope you can understand, and that our paths will cross again. I wish you only the best, and let's do whatever we need to do to make this transition a smooth one.

THE "DOWN AT HALFTIME" PEP TALK FORMULA

1. State the situation clearly and honestly—without sugar coating it.
2. State what is at stake for the company.
3. State what needs to happen.
4. State that everyone is important to this endeavor.
5. State that you will make it through.
6. Acknowledge your company's greatness.
7. Acknowledge your staff's greatness.
8. "Let's go to work and make this happen."

TEN GREAT "TOUGH TIME PEP TALK" QUOTES

It's not whether you get knocked down; it's whether you get up.

—*Vince Lombardi*

Character cannot be developed in ease and quiet. Only through experience of trial and suffering can the soul be strengthened, vision cleared, ambition inspired, and success achieved.

—*Helen Keller*

The only way around is through.

—*Robert Frost*

No pain, no palm; no thorns, no throne; no gall, no glory; no cross, no crown.

—*William Penn*

When you get to the end of all the light you know, and it's time to step into the darkness of the unknown, faith is knowing that one of two things shall happen: Either you will be given something solid to stand on, or you will be taught how to fly.

—*Edward Teller*

When things are bad, we take comfort in the thought that they could always get worse. And when they are, we find hope in the thought that things are so bad they have to get better.

—*Malcolm S. Forbes*

Big shots are only little shots who keep shooting.

—*Christopher Morley*

The strongest oak tree of the forest is not the one that is protected from the storm and hidden from the sun. It's the one that stands in the open, where it is compelled to struggle for its existence against the winds and rains and the scorching sun.

—*Napoleon Hill*

Many of life's failures are men who did not realize how close they were to success when they gave up.

—*Thomas Edison*

You know, when you get old in life, things get taken from you. That's part of life. But you only learn that when you start losing stuff. You find out that life is just a game of inches. The inches we need are everywhere around us. They are in every break of the game, every minute, every second. On this team, we fight for that inch. On this team, we tear ourselves, and everyone around us, to pieces for that inch. We claw with our fingernails for that inch. 'Cause we know when we add up all those inches, that's going to make the fucking difference between winning and losing—between living and dying.

—*Tony D'Amato (Al Pacino),* Any Given Sunday

THE RULES OF GOOD NEGOTIATION

1. Remember that the best negotiation is a win–win negotiation in which both parties get all of what they need (and some of what they want).

2. Understand as much as possible about what it is the other side needs, and what the other side wants, before sitting down together.

3. Understand what it is that you need and what you want before sitting down together.

4. Never sit down at a negotiation table from which you cannot get up.

THE FOUR BUSINESS EXIT STRATEGIES

Proper Acquisition

Managed Legacy

Head for the Hills

Emergency Sell-Off

QUICK CASH GENERATION TACTIC #1

Expert Adviser

Shawn Casey, www.shawncasey.com

This system has worked repeatedly for companies in a huge variety of markets and will certainly work for you if you follow the steps and work diligently to get companies to do the promotions for you. By the way, you obviously don't have to wait until you have a dire need for cash to use this strategy. You can do this whenever you want!

Create an absolutely killer offer for your top selling product(s) that is so good no one can reasonably fail to buy.

Create a sense of urgency by limiting the quantity of either the main product or the bonuses, and by limiting the timeframe during which the offer is available.

3 Set the offer up on a Web site, and compile a series of three e-mails that promote the offer. You will also need to set up a way to track promotions by different companies. You can do this by setting up different Web pages and/or product codes for each company, or by using an online affiliate program.

4. Contact every company you can find that would have an e-mail list of prospects and/or customers related to your market, including companies that you think of as direct competitors. (Contact any company whose list has an "opt-in" feature to their list on their Web site or mentions an online newsletter or e-zine.)

5. Tell the companies you have contacted that you have created a special offer that you feel would be well received by their prospects and customers. Briefly explain the offer as well as your company's background and credentials that show why this company should feel comfortable doing business with you and recommending you to their contacts. Ask them to promote the offer to their list via e-mail (using an e-mail that you have already prepared for them), and that you'll pay them 15 to 30 percent of the profits for each sale made through their networks. In short, if the company sends a couple of e-mails, you can quickly reward them with a large check.

6. As companies respond to your requests, encourage them to promote as soon as possible. Tell them that three mailings will produce the optimum results. After someone has sent out the first mailing, contact them with their results so they understand how much money they have already made so that they will be excited about mailing a second and third time.

QUICK CASH GENERATION TACTIC #2

Expert Adviser

Tellman Knudson, www.listbuilding.com

---

1. Set an ambitious financial goal and triple it. For example, the amount of money you need to make in order to wash-out your debt. When you do this it will help you outline a clear goal that will allow you to pay your partners, eliminate your debt, and leave you with plenty of additional cash to grow your business.

2. Identify a subject you can speak of or teach that is current and hot, that you can enlist others to speak of as well, and that has a broad, paying, audience.

Make a list of at least 50 speakers for your teleseminar series. The speakers should all fit the following criteria:

- They have an e-mail list of a minimum of 10,000 subscribers.
- They have a product to sell that costs at least $497.
- They have affiliate programs already in place that pay out a minimum of 30 percent.
- They have successfully spoken from stage before.

4. Call and e-mail all potential speakers in one day. Be sure to copy all 50 speakers on your e-mail, and let them know that the first 12 to respond will be chosen to be involved in your teleseminar series. Tell them that there is no compensation, but that they will get great promotion for their products. Be sure to set up affiliate deals with your speakers.

5. Set up your domain and squeeze page for your teleseminar series and schedule people in, based on the speed of their response.

6. Make sure all 12 speakers agree to send three e-mails to their contact list inviting them to the seminar.

7. Enlist four extra speakers as backups in case any of your speakers flake out.

8. Perform your teleseminar series for free, but immediately sell the recordings and transcripts as a one-time offer immediately after people register for your call.

9. You will make a huge surge of cash from sales of the recordings and transcripts, and then cash will continue to flow in as a result of the affiliate sales generated.

ABOUT THE EXPERTS

Working with some of the best marketers in the world, **Del Breckenfeld** developed a groundbreaking promotional program for Anheuser-Busch. From there he was able to reach the pinnacle of Fender Musical Instruments Corp. where, as director of entertainment marketing, he has been encouraged to expand his division's traditional boundaries. To learn more, visit www.fender.com and www.officialcoolfactor.com.

Chris Brogan is president of New Marketing Labs, LLC, and blogs at www.chrisbrogan.com. He is coauthor of the book *Trust Agents* and author of *The Social Media 100*. He lives on planes, but does laundry in northern Massachusetts.

Shawn M. Casey, J.D., is the author and publisher of numerous training courses primarily focused on Internet marketing including "Mining Gold On the Internet" (over 100,000 copies sold), "9 Easy Steps to Internet Cash," "Internet Law Compliance System," the "Internet Breakthrough Strategies Workshop," "How to Make a Fortune in the Information Products Business," and "List Pros." He has more than 200,000 customers in 119 countries who have benefited from his cutting edge information. To learn more, visit www.shawncasey.com.

Dr. Debra Condren is a business psychologist, the founder and president of Manhattan Business Coaching, and author of *Ambition Is Not a Dirty Word*. To learn more, visit www.businesspsychologysolutions.com.

CEO and cofounder of John Paul Mitchell Systems, **John Paul DeJoria**, with hairstylist Paul Mitchell, converted a partially borrowed $750 into the largest privately held salon hair-care line, with profits of $900 million. DeJoria is also founder and owner of Patrón Spirits Company, that accounts for more than 70 percent of sales in the ultra-premium tequila category. To learn more, visit www.paulmitchell.com.

Roxanne Emmerich, president and CEO of the Emmerich Group, is America's most sought-after workplace transformation expert. She is listed by Sales and Marketing Management magazine as one of the twelve most requested speakers in the country for her ability to transform negative workplace performance and environments into "bring it on" results-oriented cultures. Her new book, *Thank God It's Monday*, is a *New York Times*, *Wall Street Journal*, and Amazon #1 best seller. To learn more, visit www.thankgoditsmonday.com.

Michael Fishman has advised business leaders on marketing, product positioning, and work-culture subjects for more than twenty years, with expertise in health and personal development. Consultant to some of the largest direct-marketing successes in the history of publishing, Fishman facilitates the annual Consumer Health Summit, which he established in 1994. He was the only guest speaker at the historic Gary Bencivenga 100 Seminar and has been interviewed by Joe Polish for the Genius Network Series, marketing educator Ken McCarthy for the System Seminar, and consultant Perry Marshall for his Renaissance Club. To learn more, visit www.michaelfishman.wordpress.com

Jon Gordon is a speaker, consultant, and author of several books, including the international best seller *The Energy Bus: 10 Rules to Fuel Your Life, Work, and Team with Positive Energy* and *Training Camp*. He works with organizations to develop positive leaders, engaged employees, and winning teams and is sought after by many of the nation's top companies, NFL coaches, schools, and nonprofits. To learn more, visit www.jongordon.com.

Mike Hill is founder of Janta Ki Seva Inc., a boutique agency dedicated to helping humanity. By mixing cutting-edge technology and timeless advertising methods, Mike has helped those with a "calling" find the "masses" they are destined to help. With a focus on ethical marketing and transparency, Mike has led the charge in advertising with responsibility and compassion for the customer. Mike's management style has helped empower through a common goal, the betterment of humanity through service. His belief is that through profit we can aid in the redistribution of education, motivation, and mental preparedness. To learn more, visit www.mikehillsblog.com.

Kevin Hogan, Psy.D., is a professional corporate speaker whose focus is persuasion and influence; his most requested presentations concern body language and nonverbal communication. Hogan is the author of 19 books, including the international best seller *The Psychology of Persuasion*. His most recent book is *The 12 Factors of Business Success*. To learn more, visit www.kevinhogan.com/worstcasescenario.htm.

Spike Humer, CEO of Spike Humer International, is a highly successful entrepreneur, speaker, author, and performance consultant. He has coached, counseled, consulted, and taught individuals and businesses in more than 23 countries and has appeared on the same programs as such notable speakers as Jay Abraham, Mark Joyner, Chet Holmes, Mark Victor Hansen, T. Harv Eker, Stephen M. R. Covey, and many other industry thought-leaders. Widely regarded as a world-leading expert on business and personal change, Humer is author of the *The 10-Day Turnaround for Business* and developer of "The 10 Day Life Turnaround" seminar and book series. To learn more, visit www.spikehumer.com.

Dean Hunt is a young entrepreneur from the United Kingdom known worldwide as one of the most outrageous and exciting marketers. He coaches professionals on how to stand out, get more clients, and earn more profits, and his wacky branding of Killer Bunnies is the tip of the iceberg for his out-of-the-box thinking. Hunt has been described as everything from "creative genius" to "marketing hooligan." Find out more at www.deanhunt.com and www.buzzprofits.com or e-mail contact@deanhunt.com.

Caleb Jennings is a high-energy entrepreneur with a unique ability to identify and capitalize on synergistic ventures. He truly has a passion for people, networking, creating profitable partnerships and connecting the right people. The technical term for what Caleb does is "Joint Venture Management," however, friends call him the "JV Ninja." Working with marketing legends such as Joe Sugarman, Mark Joyner, and Eben Pagan, his edge is constantly being sharpened. Caleb has an appetite for adventure, participating in extreme sports worldwide such as snowboarding, skydiving, freestyle gymnastics, and has been a martial artist since age 3. Visit his personal blog at www.calebjennings.com to learn more.

Born in rural New Hampshire with twisted legs, **Tellman Knudson** is "The Backwoods Millionaire," well known for achieving the impossible in record time. At the age of 16, he defied his doctors' predictions, setting the record for speed on his cross-country course and going on to run ultra-marathons. A self-made multi-millionaire before age 30, his company, Overcome Everything, Inc., went from zero to 4.5 million a year in under three years. Recognized worldwide as the authority on Internet Listbuilding, Tellman is currently training to run barefoot across America, to raise money for teenage homelessness.

Dan Kuschell is the secret weapon of many of today's biggest marketers in business. He has been responsible for implementing campaigns generating more than $50 million for his clients. Kuschell provides consulting, coaching, and a wealth of resources for business owners at www.prosperitybasedliving.com and www.dankuschell.com.

Ryan Lee is an entrepreneur who has gone from being a gym teacher to currently running more than 100 different Internet companies and Web sites. He is author of *The Millionaire Workout* and is a highly sought after speaker and marketing coach. He publishes free training videos and articles that are seen by some 200,000 people every day at www.ryanlee.com.

Andrew Lock is the presenter of "Help! My Business Sucks!" a free weekly Web show that helps entrepreneurs "get more done and have more fun" (www.helpmybusiness.com). With his irreverent, entertaining, and humorous style, Lock provides small-business owners with practical marketing tips, lessons from well-known brands, and little-known, helpful resources. He is on a mission to expose traditional marketing techniques as outdated and ineffective and has popularized the phrase "Marketing is everything and everything is marketing."

Scott Lorenz is president of Westwind Communications, a public relations and marketing firm. As a seasoned publicist, he works with doctors, lawyers, inventors, authors, start-ups, and entrepreneurs and is often called upon in the early stages of a company's existence to get them "on the radar." As a book marketing expert, Lorenz is consulted by top executives and best-selling authors to promote their books. His clients have been featured by *Good Morning America*, *FOX & Friends*, *CNN*, *ABC Nightly News*, ESPN, *The New York Times*, *Nightline*, *TIME*,

PBS, NPR, and *USA Today*. Visit www.westwindcos.com.

Andrew Miller is president of ACM Consulting, Inc. and helps clients increase profit and operate more efficiently by aligning processes, people, and technology. For more than a decade, Miller has been providing operational and procurement advice to companies around the globe. Referred to as the Procurement Guru™, Miller has been featured in numerous national and international publications and is an active speaker and writer. Before starting his own business, he held various senior consulting positions with IBM Global Business Services and PriceWaterhouseCoopers Consulting. To learn more, visit www.acmconsulting.ca or email andrew@acmconsulting.ca.

Greg Pain is director and principal biomechanist of bioSPORT, a biomechanical sports-conditioning practice in Auckland, New Zealand. Now, with a young family of two girls—Amalie (age 3 1/2, going on 35) and Mieke (9 months)—and his lovely wife, Wendy, he has thrown himself into bioSPORT, where he and his team of physiotherapists, Pilates instructors, and biomechanists work passionately to provide not only the best possible injury-prevention and performance-enhancement training but also a level of service more akin to high-end hospitality, where personality, respect, and individuality are paramount. To learn more, visit www.biosport.co.nz.

Kerry Patterson is coauthor of three *New York Times* best sellers: *Crucial Conversations*, *Crucial Confrontations*, and *Influencer: The Power to Change Anything*. He is also a sought-after speaker and consultant and cofounder of VitalSmarts, an innovator in corporate training and organizational performance. To learn more, visit www.lifetips.com/expert-guru/6189-kerry-patterson.html.

Corey Perlman is the author of the Amazon #1 best seller *eBoot Camp: Proven Internet Marketing Techniques to Grow Your Business*. He has conducted the eBoot Camp presentation to audiences worldwide and continues to speak on the topics of Internet marketing and social media. To learn more, visit www.ebootcampbook.com.

Dr. Joe Rubino is CEO of the Center for Personal Reinvention and a personal-development trainer and certified success coach. He is the author of nine best-selling books on the achievement of personal and business success. As codeveloper of the life-changing course *Conversations for Success*, Dr. Rubino provides participants with the tools to maximize their self-esteem, productivity, and effectiveness with others. To learn more, visit www.selfesteemsystem.com and www.centerforpersonalreinvention.com.

Ric Thompson has started, purchased, and sold multiple businesses over the past decade. Currently he's a full-time Internet marketer and publisher with multiple free online magazines, notably smallbusiness ceomagazine.com and www.healthywealthynwise.com. To get the coolest small-business ideas on the planet, visit www.smallbusiness ceomagazine.com.

Dr. Joe Vitale is the author of *Attract Money Now*, *Zero Limits*, *There's a Customer Born Every Minute*, and *The Key*. He has also starred in the movies *The Secret*, *The Opus*, and *The Compass*. He is the creator of Hypnotic Writing, Hypnotic Marketing, and Miracles Coaching. To learn more, visit www.joevitale.com.

Richard Webster is the author of 98 books, including *Seven Secrets to Success*. His books have been translated into 29 languages and have sold more than 10 million copies worldwide. To learn more, visit Richard Webster, www.richardwebster.co.nz.

Lee Witt is a businessman, musician, and athlete who has worked in the research and development branch of Boeing Commercial Airplanes for 23 years. In addition to his aerospace work, Witt also trains corporations, organizations, and schools in the principles of high performance, emotional intelligence, and goal attainment. His clients include the Robert Half Company, Volt Placement Services, the University of Puget Sound, and the Society of Women Engineers. In 2008 he wrote *Become Unstoppable: Take a Different Stance in Life to Stand Up, Stand Out, and Deliver Your Best*, which outlines the eight key components for developing an unstoppable human. In addition, Witt leads one of the West Coast's most popular nightclub acts, the BrickHouse Band. To learn more, visit www.brickhouseband.com.

INDEX

ABOUT THE AUTHORS

David Borgenicht is the creator and coauthor of all books in the Worst-Case Scenario series (visit www.worstcase scenarios.com to learn more), several of which have become international best sellers. The Worst-Case Scenario books have sold more than 8 million copies, spawned board games and a television series, and been translated into more than 25 different languages. He is also founder of Quirk Books (www.quirkbooks.com), publishers of crossover nonfiction and "irreference" books. He believes firmly that there are no stupid ideas—but that there are ideas that just may not be stupid enough.

In David's words:
"The most amazing thing to me is that I get paid for doing this."

Mark Joyner is the founder and chairman of Construct Zero (www.ConstructZero.org). He is the author of more than a dozen books that have been translated into 21 languages and is widely recognized as the most influential figure in the birth of the Internet as a marketing weapon. (He and his companies having invented, popularized, and pioneered many of the technologies and conventions that are taken for granted today in the e-commerce world, including remotely hosted ad tracking, e-books, integration marketing, and more . . .).

In Mark's words:

"These days I'm more interested in entrepreneurialism as a tool for social change, and in how technology can add more bliss to our day-to-day lives. That's what Construct Zero is all about."

ACKNOWLEDGMENTS

No great book would exist without the efforts of a great team supporting it, and this book, though it may or may not be great, is no exception. We would like to thank the following players, without whom the creation of this survival guide would have been a much more dangerous undertaking: Matt Holt and Shannon Vargo and the entire crew at Wiley; Mary Ellen Wilson, Jenny Kraemer, Sarah O'Brien, and freelance designer Karen Onorato on the Quirk Productions team; Paula Uy and everyone else on the Construct Zero team; all the experts who contributed their knowledge and experience to making this book into a great resource; and, finally, all the entrepreneurs who have ever faced worst-case scenarios in business, fought back, and come out on top.

FREE 5-DAY WORST-CASE SCENARIO BUSINESS SURVIVAL COURSE

Can animated cartoons and hilarious quizzes be the hidden key to saving your business and positioning it for success?

Dear Friend,

Let's face it—most of us don't really apply what we learn in books to our lives. This book is great because you can (and should) keep it near your desk as a reference to bail you out of a jam. But what if you were able to absorb these ideas (and more) so that you didn't have to look anything up? You just knew?

One of my companies, Simpleology, does just that. We, among other things, create courseware that is based on cutting-edge learning psychology to ensure that you learn (really learn) the material as quickly as possible. What makes it even better is that at the core of these lessons are fun (and surprisingly deep) animated cartoons to make the process really enjoyable.

We've put together a 5-Day Crash Course to give you a taste of this experience—based on the material inside *The Worst-Case Scenario Business Survival Guide*. At the end of these 5 days, you'll have mastered the 5 most important things every business owner must know (but usually doesn't). You can grab it right here, and it's totally free:

www.worstcasebusiness.com

All the best,

Mark Joyner
#1 Best-Selling Coauthor of the Book You're Holding in Your Hands

P.S. Hey, Dave here—I snuck this in after Mark left. Can I tell you the truth? The courses that Mark's Simpleology puts together are, well . . . really good. Don't let Mark catch me saying this in public since it will blow up his already inflated ego, but there you go. I said it. Go snag it.